MIXED PASTURE

MIXED PASTURE

Twelve Essays and Addresses

BY

EVELYN UNDERHILL

Essay Index Reprint Series

WIPF & STOCK • Eugene, Oregon

Wipf and Stock Publishers
199 W 8th Ave, Suite 3
Eugene, OR 97401

Mixed Pasture
Twelve Essays and Addresses
By Underhill, Evelyn
ISBN 13: 978-1-4982-3430-6
Publication date 7/14/2015
Previously published by Books for Libraries Press, 1933

TO

MARGARET CROPPER

WITH LOVE AND GRATITUDE

PREFACE

THE essays and addresses collected in this book cover a period of about twelve years, and were first composed for many different purposes. Thus it is that they deal with various and even contrasting aspects of Christian spirituality, and also represent different moments in the development of their writer's thought. The earliest are the three papers on Christian social action; the latest is the study of the spiritual significance of the Oxford Movement. Yet I hope that any superficial appearance of contradiction between the pages which deal respectively with the most interior, and with the most practical expressions of the life of the spirit, will be successfully resolved by those readers who know how to browse with discrimination but without fastidiousness; going both in and out to find pasture.

Such herbage as I have to offer seems to belong to three main types, and has been arranged accordingly. The three essays which are placed first are intended to present from three angles the general principles on which all the rest are based. 'The Philosophy of Contemplation' is an attempt to describe in elementary terms the intellectual sanctions of mystical religion. It contains—with some additions—the Counsell Memorial Lecture, which I had the honour to deliver at

Cheltenham Ladies' College in 1930; and which was afterwards privately printed. 'A Study of Sanctity', which appears in its present shape for the first time, embodies a short article which was printed in the *Spectator*. It presents the same essential truths; as they are manifested in action in the life of spiritual genius. 'Spiritual Life', which is based on an address given to a group of Harrow masters, considers them again; in relation to our average human experience.

The three following addresses were delivered respectively at Swanwick, Birmingham and Oxford, during that period of awakening interest in the social implications of Christianity which had its chief expression in the 'Copec' movement. These are printed exactly as they were delivered. Their reappearance at the present time may perhaps serve as a reminder of how much which was then promised and hoped for still waits to be performed; and how shamefully Christian corporate action lags behind Christian ideals. 'Some Implicits of Christian Social Reform', and 'The Will of the Voice'—which was intended to introduce the Copec report on 'The Nature of God'—were afterwards printed in the *Pilgrim*: a magazine which no longer exists. Ten years separates the earliest paper of this group from the two last essays in the section which I have named 'Practices': those on the spiritual significance and accomplishment of the Tractarian revival, and on the inward dispositions which alone can make the present movement towards extending the sphere of women's religious work sane and fruitful. The first of these was delivered as a lecture before the Newcastle Theological Society and afterwards printed in the *Hibbert Journal*. It is an attempt to estimate the extent in which the Oxford Movement brought back to Anglican Church life the undying fundamentals of Christian spirituality. The paper on the Ministry of Women was read as the closing address at a Conference, called by the Central Council for Women's Church Work, to consider this subject. It is intended as a reminder that these same fundamentals must or should govern all experiments made in this field, if they are to contribute to the genuine enrichment of the Church's life. This paper, which is printed as delivered, has already appeared in *Theology*.

Finally, four essays deal with great and varying expressions of the spiritual life in terms of human personality; three belonging to the medieval, one to the modern world. The lecture on 'St. Francis of Assisi and Franciscan Spirituality' was delivered, under the auspices of the British Society for Franciscan Studies, at University College, London, in January 1933; as the second Walter Seton Memorial Lecture. I am grateful for this opportunity of expressing my deep sense of obligation for the honour accorded to me in being chosen for this office. The two following papers deal with the two most widely known of our English fourteenth-century mystics. 'Richard the Hermit' was first printed in the *Dublin Review* as a study of recent work on Richard Rolle. The address on Walter Hilton was read at a meeting held in his honour on the site of the Priory of Thurgarton, in Nottinghamshire; where much of his life was spent. The essay upon Baron von Hügel first appeared in the *Criterion* in 1932. The additional note, on his work as a spiritual teacher, was printed anonymously in the *Guardian* in the week following his death in January 1925.

I have to thank the editors of the *Hibbert Journal*, the *Criterion*, and the *Dublin Review* for kind permission to reprint articles which have already appeared in their pages; and the editors of *Theology* and the *Guardian* for friendly hospitality received.

E. U.

Whitsuntide, 1933

CONTENTS

I so love to watch cows as they browse at the borders, up against the hedges of fields. They move along, with their great tongues drawing in just only what they can assimilate ; yes —but without stopping to snort defiantly against what does not thus suit them. . . . So ought we to do.

F. von Hügel.

MIXED PASTURE

THE PHILOSOPHY OF CONTEMPLATION[1]

Philonous. Are you sure that you are right in saying that Aristotle held the life of contemplation to be a superhuman life? Was it not rather for him the life of man most fully man?

Theonas. It would be better to say that for him it was both at once; and it is precisely in this that he seems to me to have seen most deeply into our nature.

J. MARITAIN.

SUCH a title as 'The Philosophy of Contemplation' will seem to many people to beg two questions: one concerning the limitations of Philosophy, and the other, the very character of Contemplation itself. Yet not really so; for philosophy is the science of ultimate Reality, and contemplation, if it is genuine, is the art whereby we have communion with that ultimate Reality. Both then declare that the true meaning of our existence

[1] The Counsell Memorial Lecture, delivered at the Ladies' College, Cheltenham, 26 March 1930.

lies beyond us ; and both offer to lead us out towards it, by the contrasting routes of vision and of thought. If we took seriously—which of course we do not—Aristotle's definition of Man as a Contemplative Animal, that phrase alone might provide us with a good deal of food for reflection. For this precise thinker did not, with the exclusive mystic and the quietist, call man a Contemplative Spirit. He called him an animal, part of the natural order; distinguished from all other animals by what ?—the power of Contemplation. 'O God, thou art my God: early will I seek Thee'. Alone in the rich jungle of creation, we find man wanting to do that. Surely Aristotle was right in picking out this strange desire, as the decisive thing about us.

That a scrap of transient life, pinned to this tiny planet and limited by the apprehensions of its imperfect senses and the interpretations of its yet more imperfect mind, should be filled to the brim with a passion for that which lies beyond life—this, even if it only happened once, would present a difficult problem to the determinist. But it happens frequently. Philosophy has not only to make room for the intellectual experiences of a Plato, a Descartes, a Kant, a Hegel. It must also make room for the contemplative experiences of a St. Paul, a Plotinus, an Augustine, a Francis, a Teresa ; and for the fact that human life only achieves its highest levels under the direct or oblique influence of such personalities as these, and the conviction of spiritual reality and its demands which they alone seem able to convey. They give to our life something otherwise lacking, which we cannot quite get for ourselves. Although it is not a truth which we are fond of, something deep within us insists that Mary has chosen the good, the real, the noble part ; and that without her steadfast witness to the Perfection she adores, our busy life of becoming would lose all significance.

'The Contemplative life is the Vision of the Principle', says St. Gregory. Only man is capable of that vision, that discovery of the meaning of life. That is why he is a contemplative animal ; why it is the good part, and without it there is a cleavage in his life, the fatal cleavage between idea and act.

Of course Contemplation, thus understood, means something far more fundamental than the special kind of devotion which is often called by that name in ascetic books. It means that spiritual realism, that concrete hold on the Reality of God, without which religion is hardly more than the beneficent illusion which Freud supposes it to be. It means what von Hügel called our sense of Eternal Life. 'Every man as such', said William Law, 'has an open gate to God in his soul.' Philosophy merely puts this in its own language, when it says that man is capable of the intuition of absolutes. Religion is stating the same thing in lovelier words, when it declares that the pure in heart can see God. The link between all these sayings, then, is their insistence that human personality has about it something which is not accounted for by nature, and is not satisfied by nature. We do not belong to the world of succession alone. Deeply immersed though our lives may seem to be in that world of succession, we are yet able to know the Unchanging; and when we forget this, at once those lives are out of shape. 'Ye are of God, little children.' There is within us the seed of absolute life. Therefore in man 'most fully man', correctly adjusted to reality, contemplation, the Vision of the Principle—in other words, spiritual realism—would be the true cause of all action. There should be no cleavage between them.

Here then we have a doctrine which is embedded in the very substance of Christian philosophy: a doctrine which, if we took it seriously, must affect not only our philosophy but our psychology too, and not only these abstract studies, but our whole conduct of life. It would determine our social structures, our educational aims; and movement towards its more perfect actualization would be the only progress worthy of the name. In spite of the so-called revival of mysticism, however, I do not think any one will contend that this doctrine *is* now taken seriously either by philosophy or by religion. We talk and write easily and freely about spiritual values and the spiritual life; but we remain fundamentally utilitarian, even pragmatic, at heart. We want spiritual things to work; and the standard we apply is our miserable little notion of how they ought to work. We always want to know whether they are helpful. Our philosophy and religion are orientated, not towards the awful Vision of that Principle before which Isaiah saw the seraphim veil their eyes; but merely towards the visible life of man and its needs. We may speak respectfully of Mary, and even study her psychology; but we feel that the really important thing is to encourage Martha to go on getting the lunch. Yet the whole witness of religious history supports St. Luke and Aristotle and St. Gregory. Understood in the deepest and widest sense, Contemplation is the very life blood of religion. It is and has ever been the one thing needful, 'the life of man most fully man'. Be still and *know* that I am God. It cannot be done in any other way. It is true that he who runs may read ; but he cannot so easily observe the stars.

So here is something which the religious philosopher cannot neglect. It is his duty to heal the conflict between practical life and contemplative life. He must remind our institutional and philanthropic Marthas that the whole sanction for their activities—the only reason why religion exists at all—abides in the fact that men and women do possess a sense of God, of Eternal Life; that they are contemplative animals. That one fact lies at the root of all creeds, all churches, all prayer. It is, in fact, one of the key-pieces in the intricate puzzle of our mental and spiritual life. It is a very awkwardly shaped piece for the intellectualist and for the naturalist ; but we have got to find its place in the scheme. It is true that we cannot yet make it fit quite neatly. For this, we need much further knowledge of our own many-levelled mental life on one hand, and of the relation between different kinds of knowledge—spiritual, intellectual and aesthetic—on the other hand. But that is no reason for leaving it in the box ; and ignoring the plain fact that it is one of the most important pieces in the religious complex, and may yet prove the clue to the whole pattern of life. Whatever we choose to call it, it represents the most distinctive and unquenchable of all man's passions, the strangest of his endowments; what Plotinus called his Sense of the Yonder. Thus our whole philosophy of life must be conditioned by the position we give to it; and Christianity, though so much more than a philosophy of life, must have a philosophic scheme, and must make that scheme wide enough and deep enough to accommodate the largest possible number of religious experiences and facts. It is from this point of view that modern philosophies of religion often seem rather thin, tight and academic; terribly inadequate to the profound experiences of the Saints, who are after all our chief sources of information, the seers, explorers, artists, great navigators of the Ocean of God.

If we do not dismiss them as mere aberrations—and psychology is finding it more and more difficult to do this—the facts of the contemplative life, both in its general diffuse manifestations and its vivid embodiments, involve certain theological and philosophical consequences. The Abbé Bremond, who has devoted two volumes of his great *Histoire Littéraire* to the history and psychology of this subject, speaks without scruple of the 'metaphysic of the saints'. And the true peculiarity of the 'metaphysic of the saints' is the fact that it is controlled by the fruits of contemplation, the certainty of first-hand contact with a spiritual reality that is beyond but not against reason. Therefore a central place in Christian philosophy—indeed, in any really spiritual philosophy—must be left for this strange passion, this peculiar way of knowledge; we cannot avoid our obligations by sending its best products to the convent, and its worst to the asylum. But far more thought and exploration than we have given it yet lies before those who want to harmonize this department of human experience with the rest. The best modern work on this subject, and on the psychology of religious experience—which is all part of it,—suggests that we are at last beginning to move towards a more satisfactory theory of contemplation than any held in the past generation by those who explored it either from the direction of religion or the direction of science; one which will interpret tradition in the light of experience, and bring us nearer to an understanding of the close relation between religious truth and poetic truth. The most important part of this work has been done in France: by the Abbé Bremond, whose remarkable essay on 'Prayer and Poetry' is now widely known, by the psychologist and theologian Maréchal, and by the philosopher Jacques Maritain. Yet this work is, to a large extent, the recovery and re-statement of doctrine once generally held by spiritual men, and found to be endorsed by their experience.

What then do we mean by Contemplation? What is it? When we have considered this, we may see more clearly its place in our view of the human mind and its workings—psychology: and our view of the nature of reality—philosophy. I take it that, in the widest sense, we mean by Contemplation the human self's method of stretching out towards truth which lies beyond and above his reason; his communion with a reality which is not given us by the senses, or reached by logical thought. Though it may include the sort of pantheistic reverie sometimes called Nature Mysticism, real Contemplation goes far deeper than this; for its true object is that mysterious Something Other, the Holy and Unchanging, which gives meaning to life. If we take our stand by the contemplative and ask how life seems to him, he will probably say, in his own special language, that it seems to him to be a shifting, intricate half-real process, over against Something Else, transfused by Something Else, which is not shifting but is wholly real: something abiding, fully given, prevenient, as theology would say. He will add, that for him the visible world derives all its significance from that Something Else; and that the hours in which he has communion with It are, as St. Gregory has it, 'alone the true refreshment of the mind'. At moments, of course—as St. Augustine says in 'the flash of a hurried glance'—all, or nearly all, of us, tend to see existence like that. Therefore the contemplative experience is something which we ought not to find it difficult to believe in; even though our own share in it be faint or rare.

When we consider such crumbs of spiritual experience as have been vouchsafed to us, or look at the general witness of the race, we see that at a certain level of consciousness, this sort of apprehension always tends to emerge. There is a pause in our normal useful busy correspondence with the world of use and wont. Another inhabitant comes to the window of the soul; and looks with awe and joy upon another landscape, seen because sought, and possessed because desired. We all know, that is to say, however badly we express it and however firmly we ignore it, that there is a certain duality in our life : we are not truly one, but truly two. 'In the course of the normal development of man', says Bremond, 'there occur moments in which the discursive reason gives place to a higher activity, imperfectly understood and indeed at first disquieting.' This higher activity—this hidden inhabitant—is intuitive rather than logical in its methods. It knows by communion, not by observation. It cannot give a neat account of its experience : for this experience overflows all categories, defies all explanations, and seems at once self-loss, adventure, and perfected love. If we attempt to analyse and pigeon-hole what it gives us, we ruin it at once. But if we accept the evidence it forces on us we have to allow that there are two kinds of real knowledge accessible to man. One kind of knowledge is like seeing within a narrow, but sharply focussed area. The other kind of knowledge is more like bathing in a fathomless ocean, or breathing an intangible and limitless air. It gives contact and certitude, but not understanding : as breathing or bathing give us certitude about the air and the ocean, but no information about their chemical constitution.

Experience as a whole supports this distinction of two quite different capacities in man ; two different ways of getting two different sets of knowledge. We commonly call one rational, and the other intuitive ; one logical and the other poetic ; one doctrinal, the other devotional. But these words merely advertise our ignorance. Experience is perpetually hinting that we are far more mysteriously compounded than psychology will yet acknowledge ; that we have, as human beings, contact with many levels of reality. In moments of heightened sensitiveness, and especially under the peculiar influence of aesthetic feeling—which still awaits explanation from naturalistic psychology—the psyche loosens its frenzied grip on the obvious world and becomes aware—dimly yet most vividly—of deeper, richer, more universalized realities than the logical reason can reach. But the fullest awakening of this faculty, the most intense, awestruck, and delighted apprehension of Absolutes, remains the special prerogative of religion. The peculiar activity of religion which we call in its widest sense prayer, and in its intense form contemplation, is orientated towards this. And wherever men are religious at all, this activity arises and this power is developed with more or less completeness.

Nor are we to think of this Reality as less concrete, less rich, more thin and abstract, than the world of our sensory experience. The vision of the Principle, however vague and dim our sight, is the vision of Absolute Plenitude, of All that is. 'O! the depth of the riches!' cries St. Paul. Such dimness and vagueness as accompany our contact with it, and such contradictions as occur in the descriptive efforts of the mystics, striving to reconcile the extremes of amazement and love, must be attributed to our uncertain touch, our still embryonic spiritual sense. Hence too the tension, and sometimes abnormal mentality, which accompany these adventures upon the very frontiers of the human world. Yet when even the fullest allowance has been made for all this, and for the fact that here man's reach must ever exceed his grasp; how impressive is the combined witness of corporate and personal religion to the realistic character of its Object, and the breadth and height and depth of that region to which the soul attains in contemplation.

It is strange that the immense importance of these facts has not been more generally realized: for here we lay our finger on the organ of man's spiritual knowledge. We use the word Spiritual easily and lightly. Yet, if we look at it with detachment, what a queer word it is—what a queer concept it is—for the human animal to have achieved. So useless, indeed meaningless, from the naturalistic point of view; yet entwined in all that we feel most valid, most worth having in life. If we were suddenly asked to define what we meant by the word Spiritual, most of us would feel as baffled as St. Augustine when he was asked to define Time. We too know what it is, until we are asked to describe it. For this is a word that stands for the Something Other, sought and found in human religion: and, more than this, for a whole range of most real and deep demands and activities, set towards the unchanging and away from the changeful surface of our life. We are constantly compelled to resort to it, in order to find a place for the richest and loveliest developments of that life; for it is just these developments that elude all rational explanation. Heroic sanctity, the instinct of sacrifice, the redemptive power of suffering: these solid facts are quite incompatible with naturalism but entirely harmonious with the world of spiritual reality to which the soul tends in contemplation.

If we put this view of human experience side by side with the scientific view of human experience, what does it require of us, in the way of an enlargement of our conception of the nature of man? What adjustments of psychology does it involve? Surely the first question which it forces upon us is this: Is there indeed a faculty, a way of knowledge, in man, distinct from the senses and from discursive and conceptual thought, which can give us genuine knowledge of a sort that cannot ever be obtained by means of the senses or of discursive thought? Is the contemplative or poetical consciousness something distinct from ordinary consciousness? When Keats uttered that celebrated, but much misunderstood and rather badly worded aspiration, 'O for a life of sensation rather than thought!' was he merely desiring agreeable aesthetic feeling, or was he reaching out to a direct but dimly understood communion with the reality of things? Was he being very superficial, or very profound? However differently they frame or justify their answers, poets, artists and saints agree that he was being very profound. It is their universal testimony that they are not only conscious of a world of reality and beauty shown to them and affecting them. They are also conscious of something else, conveyed by it, or of a distinctive state or condition in themselves; a sort of life, usually latent, which has been stirred to activity. They may describe it in various ways, but all make plain this two-fold character of their fullest knowledge.

Stated in its most absolute and provocative form, this means that Man has not only a natural but a supernatural environment ; and not only a supernatural environment, but also a supernatural life : that he already belongs to the world of Being as well as the world of Becoming, and under certain conditions can enter here and now into his double heritage. Keats, I think, had discovered and was trying to express this two-fold character of human consciousness : for he knew that the secret roots of poetry, as of religion, were planted in the world to which he had access in that generalized awareness, that quiet receptive state which he unfortunately called, because he could find no better term for it, 'sensation rather than thought'. He meant the same thing as that very different poet Matthew Arnold, when he said it was the peculiar privilege of poetry to give us 'a wonderfully full, new, and intimate sense' of contact with the real life of things.

That saying, translated to the theological level, conveys more accurately than many disquisitions on mysticism, the character of contemplation. It gives a full, new, intimate sense of contact with *real* life : in this case, the life of spiritual things. It confers poetic, not scientific, knowledge of God. Not by way of thought, but by way of a willed yet passive receptivity. Not through the logical mind, or the stimulation of the senses ; but through something else. So the poet and the contemplative stand side by side—Plotinus and Coleridge, Keats and St. John of the Cross—witnessing each in their own manner to an immense tract of human experience which is commonly ignored, or at best indulgently allowed by us. And yet this is the most significant and most characteristic part of human experience ; for here man discloses his transcendental nature, his inherent power of desiring and discerning Eternal Life, his passion for absolutes, for God, the Supreme Object of philosophy and religion.

And this cloud of witnesses requires of psychology, that it finds room somehow for the distinction which was first stated by the Platonists, and on which 'spiritual' persons have insisted ever since: the distinction between a 'higher' and a 'lower' self in man, that 'somewhat' in him which—however he defines it—is capable of eternity, and that natural being he shares with the animal world. 'There is a root or depth in thee', says William Law. 'This depth is the unity, the eternity, I had almost said the infinity of thy soul, for it is so infinite that nothing can satisfy it or give it any rest, but the infinity of God.' What we call contemplation is simply the activity of this fundamental hidden self ; reserved, silent, but now and then emerging in response to every stimulus which has in it the savour of the Infinite. Even though we never get a clear and steady conception of it—for the soul, as Claudel says, is silent when the mind looks at it—we all know in our own experience that this distinction answers to facts. Martha and Mary do live together in the house of the soul. One is absorbed in multiplicity ; the other is gathered into unity. Martha, the extrovert, is busy and loquacious. Mary, the introvert, keeps her secret to herself. One acts, the other adheres. Together they witness to the two-fold action of the psyche; and the two-fold character of that world, both temporal and eternal, in which the psyche is placed. To ignore this duality is to impoverish our view of human nature, and I doubt whether psychology in the true sense is going to establish itself on a firm basis until it consents to recognize this. Nor will practical human life, which is after all psychology expressed in action, achieve harmony and power till it is submitted to the same truth. The integration of prayer and action, tempering and re-inforcing each other—depth to balance expansion, and surrender to balance power—this alone can give to human life the richness of reality. Adam must return to contemplation, heal the cleavage in his nature, and accept the full destiny of a creature called to be a link between eternity and time.

I think that a study of method and result in religion, and still more plainly perhaps a study of method and result in creative art—that most fruitful field of research for the religious philosopher—helps us to establish a little more clearly the character and method of this contemplative or transcendental sense. What is the characteristic which confers greatness on a work of art? Surely the fact that in some degree it weaves together two worlds; gives sensuous expression to the fruits of contemplation, and conveys to us a certain savour of the Infinite by means of finite things. The power of conveying ecstasy, said Arthur Machen years ago, is the touchstone and secret of art; and ecstasy is simply a strong name for the release of the transcendental sense, which here communicates its results by means of material given by the senses. Thus and only thus, can we account for the peculiar stimulus which is given by great art to something in us, which ordinary arguments cannot reach: the solemn thrill of the numinous, removed perhaps at several degrees but still operative, which is felt when we stand in the Cathedral of Chartres, listen to a Beethoven symphony, or read 'The Ancient Mariner'.

Such a work of art, if it is to perform this, its essential office, requires of the artist three things. (1) The contact in his soul's deeps with the reality which lies beyond sense. (2) Its translation into symbolic forms which are accessible to the senses, and with which the rational mind can deal. (3) The energetic will, which selects, moulds and creates from this material a picture, a melody, a poem. The whole artistic and poetic process is a process of incarnation: contemplation issuing in action. Martha and Mary have collaborated in the construction of a bridge along which news from the eternal comes into the sensible world, and enters through this door the field of normal consciousness.

In this respect, the greater part of the literature of religion, and especially all that part which seeks to convey the special experiences of religion, is poetic literature. Many of our muddles and disputes about it would vanish if we would acknowledge this patent truth. Religious literature is trying to convey one thing in terms of another thing: and must do so, if it is ever to reach our minds, which, after all, are tuned-in to the wave-lengths of the visible world. It obeys, in fact, the rules of artistic creation ; and we shall appreciate it much better if we remember this. In Bremond's words, the religious writer is always at work ' turning prayer into poetry ', bringing purely spiritual material within reach of our sense-conditioned minds : and the more thoroughly he does this, the better we understand him.

Read without prejudice, such different works as St. Augustine's Confessions, the Revelations of Julian of Norwich or the Divine Dialogue of St. Catherine of Siena, make this plain to us. All these describe to us under symbols, a vision of that which in its reality lies far beyond sight and beyond symbol ; and they do this by the deliberate and selective exercise of the creative will, weaving a garment in which their vision of God can be clothed. The raw material of this garment is sure to be taken—indeed, can only be taken—from their stock of beliefs, memories, and traditions, and from their visible surroundings. In other words, apperception plays a large part in the creation of spiritual literature. Thus Ezekiel sees a vision obviously inspired by the masterpieces of Chaldean art that surround him. Yet borne upon the wings of those Living Creatures, he truly apprehends the power and the splendour of God. Thus John in Patmos sees a vision for which Ezekiel provides the pictorial form ; yet within this familiar symbolism he apprehends the deeper Christian mystery of ' the Lamb that is slain from the foundation of the world '. In each case then the image, of which the provenance is so easily traced by us, is merely the carrying medium of something else : something not to be obtained by thinking, but by some other activity of the soul, and which cannot be accounted for by the operations of the surface-mind. We may say indeed of the work of the great religious artist what Professor Lowe says in that illuminating book, *The Road to Xanadu*, of the work of the great poet :

> From the empire of chaos a new tract of cosmos has been retrieved ; a nebula has been compacted—it may be—into a star.

Yet in this effort of translation, the artist—whether he is trying to give us aesthetic or religious truth—must always descend one step from the levels of contemplation ; and in doing so must leave something behind. He always knows this, and it is the tragic element in his vocation. This is equally true of the philosopher Plotinus with his strange and almost stammering hints about the Yonder, and his final cry ' He who knows this will know what I mean ' ; of the great religious genius of Augustine, frustrated and delighted by that Holy Joy of which there is nothing he can say ; of the unlettered Angela of Foligno, exclaiming ' Not this ! not this ! I blaspheme ', as she struggles to put her overwhelming experience of God into words ; of the learned mystic Tauler, driven beyond all the ordinary resources of image to speak of ' the Abyss which is unknown and has no name . . . more beloved than all that we can know.' Beethoven fighting with the limitations of sound and rhythm, Dante, at the end of the Paradiso, recognizing the utter inadequacy of the poet to the final vision of Reality—' My own wings were not fitted for this flight '—assure us by their very failure of a splendour which cannot be revealed. The poet, says Bremond, is a broken-down mystic. Better perhaps to say, a mediator, an interpreter, who brings us at his own cost the news of eternal life. One who might have had the good part of Mary, but deliberately accepts the more homely office of Martha; and dishes up some fragments of the heavenly feast for his fellow men. The heart of his experience of truth or of beauty, based as it is on an inarticulate though vivid communion—on love rather than thought—remains incommunicable; and he knows this. Nothing is more striking in the literature of contemplation, and of high aesthetic experience, than its steady and unanimous witness to an overplus, an experienced reality, a joy and richness, which can never be conveyed save by allusion. Hence its language must always have a fluid and poetic quality, must suggest more than it ventures to define; for it always points beyond itself, and carries an *aura* of suggestion. Theology becomes a dead language the moment it forgets this fact. ' Then only ', says St. Gregory, ' is there truth in what we know concerning God, when we are made sensible that we cannot know anything concerning Him '. ' There is a distance incomparable ', says à Kempis, ' between the things men imagine by natural reason, and those which illuminated men behold by contemplation.' And St. Thomas, yet more strongly: ' Divine things are not named by our intellect as they really are in themselves, for in that way it knows them not.' And Ruysbroeck: ' It is beyond ourselves that we are one with God.' Supra-rational experience ; that, however much the intellectualist and utilitarian may dislike it, is at once the paradox and life blood of religion, as it is of creative art. The saints are always telling us of contact with another level of life, which convicts, delights and transfigures them ; that ' Clear day of eternity which never changes state into its contrary '. They tell us about it very clumsily, and often by symbols which may or may not be acceptable to us ; but they always manage to convey a sense that they have had contact with Absolutes.

A church that has forgotten this, which has abandoned the transcendental temper and fallen from contemplation, has lost the meaning of its own activities. For the whole business of expressive religion—literary, ceremonial, and sacramental—is to give something of one thing, in terms of another thing. It has got to give man's deepest intuitions of a Reality which lies beyond the senses, in such a way that this can combine with the material given by the senses. To put it in strict terms, its business is the symbolic communication of Absolutes. It is called upon to bridge the gap between mystical and rational knowledge—move to and fro between Contemplation and Meditation—and for this it will need all the resources of history, of drama, of liturgical and aesthetic suggestion. Therefore a philosophy of religion which emphasizes the supra-rational character of faith, and remembers that the Church is a society of contemplative animals, can never be—as some suppose—hostile to institutions and external forms. It does not support the shallow notion that there is a necessary contrast between ceremonial and spiritual religion, by any arbitrary limitation of the materials which can be used in this great art-work of the soul. On the contrary it knows that man's craving for God and instinct for God require all possible paths of discharge—social, intellectual, ritual, traditional—if the richness of their content is to be expressed.

Such a philosophy as this, I believe, will provide the most promising and solid foundation on which to build that modern apologetic for institutional religion which the Church so badly needs. It is never the genuine mystic who talks about 'dead forms'. He can reach out, through every religious form, to that Eternal Reality which it conveys. For him, every church will be a bridge-church, and all the various experiences of religion graded and partial revelations of the Being of Beings, the one full Reality—God. Conscious of the double nature of his own experience, of the two strands which are present in that incarnate poem we call human life, he is not much troubled by the crude and imperfect means which may be used by religion to convey its ineffable truths: for the most childish and the most sophisticated images may be equally far from representing the holy reality, yet equally able to convey it. The great thing is that the conveyance should take place, and in a way that can reach a wide variety of souls. For this, he knows. it must be combined with familiar material which these souls can understand. And that means an amalgam in which there is something of spirit, and also something of sense: something divine and something human too. It means, in fact, incarnation.

If this be true, then it is surely an important function of religious exercises to release and nourish the contemplative sense ; and we obtain from this a standard by which to measure their success or failure. The church in which we breathe the very atmosphere of worship—the liturgy that enchants as well as informs—these are doing the work to which external religion is called : making a bridge between the temporal and the eternal world. This is magnificently taught by that master psychologist St. Ignatius, when he makes all the elaborate discipline of the 'Spiritual Exercises', all the moral probing, the deliberate visualizing, and detailed meditation of Scripture, fade away in the end before one thing : which he calls 'a contemplation to procure the love of God'.

Leading on from this, it seems worth while to ask what this view of the nature of contemplation, this restoration of a belief in the distinctness of Spirit, the double character of man's life, is going to do for dogmatic religion. Surely a great deal. For in the first place it calls upon theology to put the Transcendent first ; to remember that its chief business is always with God, and its abiding temper must be adoration. This is already beginning to be realized, and accounts for the enormous influence of such thinkers as Otto and Karl Barth. Though in his struggles to tell some fragments of that which he has known the contemplative often uses pantheistic language, his very reaction is a tribute to the otherness and transcendence of God. Further, his steady and awe-struck witness to the unsearchableness of the Eternal rebukes the fatuous assumption that we can make a diagram of the Divine nature, or speak with assurance about 'getting new conceptions' of Him. There is a stern realism about the greatest utterances of the mystics, which shows that the solemn dread which Otto has shown to be a part of all full experience of the Numen, enters into their deepest apprehensions of Reality. Were these reports accepted as evidence, they might help to cure the unpleasant and almost impudent familiarity which colours a certain type of popular theological writing.

Secondly, as regards the problems surrounding theological re-statement, a good many difficulties would resolve themselves if we recognized more clearly and less nervously the necessary part which is played by symbol and image in all religious formulas, and the fact that in those formulas we are always dealing with a translation, or rather paraphrase, of a text which we cannot read. For here the Thomist distinction between 'sign' and 'thing' is experienced by the soul in its extreme form.

Thirdly, this view of contemplation might lead to a better estimate of the relation between prayer and faith. For genuine prayer, as all its great initiates have insisted, is the communion of the human spirit with the Spirit of Spirits; a responsive movement towards a prevenient Reality. It is rooted in ontology: an appeal from the successive to the Abiding. Even in its crudest forms, then, it is already a sort of contemplation. Its very essence is a mysterious contact, which gives us a certain realistic experience of the Infinite: and by disciplined attention and willed self-abandonment this experience can be deepened, steadied, enhanced. Hence its witness to Reality should be accorded the respectful attention we give to any 'real existent'. The attempts of naturalistic psychology to explain it on subjective lines all break down before any honest and persistent study of its real character and achievements. Therefore what happens to us in this vast and varied world of prayer—the world of our specifically religious experience—will greatly and rightly influence our beliefs. As there can be no valid and realistic doctrine of prayer which does not rest on and involve a doctrine of God; so no doctrine of God can be adequate which does not take account, and even very great account, of the life of prayer. In prayer the soul comes nearest the experience of absolute love: in belief it ascends by means of symbols towards absolute truth. *Lex orandi lex credendi* is true, then; perhaps in a far more actual sense than those who first made that axiom supposed. It is only by a fuller entrance into this world of prayer that we obtain a standard by which to interpret religious history; which tells us of other contacts, other experiences of Eternal Life. Here alone we can develop the spiritual sympathy, the peculiar sensitiveness, which is essential to the understanding of spiritual truth: for religion, like beauty, cannot be experienced in cold blood. Dogmatic theology is largely concerned with Truth as seen from within the house of prayer and contemplation. For here, within the house, though the lighting is dim, and some of the furniture is clumsy, and much that we vaguely perceive is beyond our comprehension, we do at least realize the use of those pipes and chimney-pots which looked so queer and disconcerting from outside. Our difficulty in giving living content to our religious formulas, the dreadful sense of unreality which clings to many of the definitions of faith, arise very largely from the fact that we are thus viewing from the outside that which can only disclose its meaning when seen from within. Thus for instance, the problems of Christology entirely change their form and colour when they are viewed within this atmosphere; gaining a new mystery, beauty and depth.

Along these lines, perhaps, the modern world may be brought to realize that religion is not to be justified by the improvements it may effect in this world; but by the news that it gives of another world. It is true that when this news—this metaphysical reality—is brought into human life and becomes dominant, all our reactions to the physical are profoundly modified. The more Eternal Life permeates our mentality, the more deep and rich becomes our interpretation of temporal life, and the higher our standard of responsibility rises. And were the fusion between contemplation and action complete, the Kingdom of God—which is already within, in the ground of our personality—would be manifest in space and time. But the moment religion begins to place these practical advantages in the foreground and depart from disinterested adoration, she has cut herself off from her sources of power.

Finally, if we accept—of course under due safeguards—the central experiences of the contemplative, his claim to a certain freely given contact with Absolutes, as giving us real news about the universe; what effect will this have upon pure philosophy?

First, it is wholly incompatible, not only with any mechanistic theory of reality and any form of subjective idealism; but also with those sloppy levelling down types of monism, which seem to offer an easy (far too easy) reconciliation of religion and science, and form the back-bone of much popular apologetic. Next, as against naturalism, it presses upon us a conviction of the concrete reality and distinctness of the Supernatural. For, though the psychological accidents that often accompany contemplation may be very neatly explained by physiology, or even biochemistry, both the essential experience and its transforming results are still left over. These, if we take them seriously, force us to admit the existence of a knowledge *wholly other* in method and content than our knowledge of the natural world: a knowledge which in its wholeness impresses itself on the whole self, in so far as that self turns towards it with a receptive attention. For the contemplative experience bears its own witness to the character of God; correcting the modern emphasis on visible nature as the capital scene of His self-disclosure to man. It leads the self into a level of life other than that of nature, and shows it the rich and mysterious web of existence in spiritual regard.

Hence the genuine knowledge of Divine Immanence which grows with the deepening of man's prayer is always the knowledge of a Divine Otherness: and the constantly heard invitations to seek and find God in nature—that is to say in the physical scene, or rather our imperfect and ever-changing apprehension of the physical scene—may result in actual damage to the deepest interests of religion, if it is allowed to obscure the primacy of those revelations of an unchanging reality made only in that deep communion where the spirit ' seeks God in her ground '. For then, something enters human experience from beyond the range of sensible perception and intellectual analysis; requiring from us the acknowledgement that we, though immersed in the temporal, do live and have our being within the mysterious precincts of an eternal world, supra-sensible indeed but not wholly unknowable. Whatever guess we make about the ultimate nature of Reality, it must leave room for the fact that the fullest human experience always has this dual character. That discovery of one world in and through another world, which is the essence of sacramentalism, speaks to us as it does just because we too are double: really things of spirit and really things of sense. I do not wish to use the controversial word dualism: but only to point to some facts of experience which the monist never seems to take sufficiently seriously.

Last, when stripped of the symbolic language in which it is always conveyed to us, philosophy finds that the experience of contemplation is at bottom an experience of value: of the quality, not the quantity, of Ultimate Truth. We obtain from genuine mystical literature a united witness to the splendour, the joy, the inherent goodness of this Ultimate; and of its immanence, its insistent living pressure on the still undeveloped, half-grown consciousness of Man. Because of that experience, philosophy—and especially the philosophy of religion—cannot rest content with any theory of life and knowledge which is not sufficiently wide and deep to include and interpret St. Thomas Aquinas, as well as the last findings of naturalistic psychology. Not only that St. Thomas who so patiently classified and explained the gropings of the intellect towards God ; but the far greater and more significant St. Thomas who quietly put away his pen and parchment saying : 'I have seen too much, I can write no more.' The St. Thomas who had passed from knowledge to wisdom, and from reason to contemplation.

WHAT IS SANCTITY?

THE real nature of sanctity, all that its existence means for our view of human personality, still remains strangely ignored by the modern world. The saint is acknowledged as an exaggerated religious type, an interesting subject for psychological investigation; but seldom for that which he is—a creative genius in the spiritual sphere, whose very existence witnesses to the priority of God. Yet surely St. Paul, in his marvellous vision of the whole Christian society as the organ, the 'mystical body' of one eternal Spirit, 'dividing to every man severally as He will', gave us once for all a clue to the peculiar significance of the saints. For these are spiritual realists, self-given without condition to the purposes of God; and therefore accepting without compromise that ineffable vocation, with all that is involved in it of suffering and labour, of total and joyful subjection to the demands of 'that same God who worketh all in all'. And by one of the paradoxes which abound in the spiritual life, it is only when his life is thus given to the purposes—however strange and costly—of an abiding Perfection that lies beyond the world, that the human creature seems able to achieve such perfection as is possible within the world. For him sanctification and sacrifice are two faces of one fact. He ' partakes of the Divine nature ' in the degree in which he is self-given to it. Subdued to the pressures and the demands of that mysterious energy, Its loving and untiring friend and servant, he becomes in his turn and in his small measure a creative personality ; takes up his part in the eternal process of bringing forth within the world the life and love of God.

' Man ', says William Law, ' has a Seed of the Divine life given into the birth of his soul, a Seed that has all the riches of eternity in it, and is always wanting to come to the birth in him and be alive in God.' The flowering of that Seed is sanctity ; for the life of holiness is really part of that universal process which Christian theology means by Incarnation. It reproduces, and even continues in its measure, the life of Christ within the world ; especially that life's most awful and mysterious reaches, its energizing power and its costly redemptive action on suffering and sin. As the souls of the saints grow, and their real spiritual personality begins to appear ; so on one hand we find that their loving identity with all other souls grows too, and on the other hand that loving union with God which makes them in a special degree the friends and agents of the Eternal Charity, becomes ever deeper, more delicate, more selfless, more complete. They are possessed and devoured by the longing to help, to heal, to save. Thus the deep joy which persists through their darkest hours and utmost weariness, has nothing in common with the placid happiness of the devotee. Feeling and bearing the mysterious burden of the sins and sufferings of the world, their growth in sanctity is always a growth in meekness and in penance. That beauty of holiness which we reverence in them, they cannot see; for their eyes are fixed on the absolute Beauty and Holiness which they follow and adore. The attitude of the redeeming saint, in his simplicity and self-abasement, remains to the end the attitude of the Publican. His many reasons for thanksgiving never include his own superior state. We notice too in the best of them a certain sweetness, easiness and lack of rigorism, which comes from dying to self and its limitations: a death which is never without suffering, and must be constantly renewed. 'We see saints smiling, and persons praying peacefully', says Huvelin, 'but only just consider what is going on in the depth of their souls!'

This strange thing Holiness, this entire self-giving of the human soul to the Eternal, takes as many forms as human character itself. Some of these forms charm us; others disconcert and even repel the natural mind. All have a quality which is calculated to make that natural mind feel rather uncomfortable. For in truth the vocation of the saint is always a call to those heroic levels of existence which a bourgeois spirituality prefers to ignore; and in whatever way this call is obeyed, it casts an unbecoming light on that which Huvelin was accustomed to call our 'incurable mediocrity of soul'. It is both humbling and bracing to contemplate the self-oblivious passion and adventurous trust which wedded St. Francis to Poverty, determined the great career of St. Ignatius, laid on St. Catherine of Siena or the Curé d'Ars the holy cross of vicarious atonement, sent Bunyan to Bedford gaol, Henry Martyn to India, Foucauld to the Sahara, or Father Wainright to the lifelong service of the poor; yet more illuminating to contrast the natural equipment of these souls as they first come before us, with the mature spiritual personalities which are formed of this various raw material under the steady reciprocal action of the divine and the human love: out of its very weakness bringing fresh beauty and power.

Thus Francis, a pleasure-loving boy and natural artist, feeling to the full the natural human loathing for squalor and for hideous sights, conquers that disgust by a sublime movement of charity, and makes of it a stepping-stone to God. Ignatius, beginning as a worldly and self-indulgent young soldier, devotes that militant temper to the struggle for holiness; and is described in his last years as 'having become all love', and never making a decision without resort to God. Catherine of Genoa, a melancholy and disillusioned woman, becomes by persevering communion with the invisible Love a great philanthropist and mother of souls. Teresa, a high-spirited, romantic, passionate creature, confessed that the devil often sent her a 'spirit of bad temper' and was accustomed to refer to the unreformed and comfort-loving Carmelites as 'cats'. She comes by courage and love to the height of self-abandonment at which she can refuse the temptation to 'serve God in a corner' and renounce the very joys of contemplation, in order to obey the secret pressure which sends her out to reform the religious life of Spain. Augustine Baker, forsaking in discouragement the contemplative pathway for nine years, meekly and bravely returns to it ; and becomes in consequence one of its surest, deepest, and gentlest guides. Fénelon, the brilliant courtier and ecclesiastic, driven into disgrace by the combined results of misunderstanding and jealousy, humbly devotes himself to the self-occupied penitents who pursue him with their ceaseless letters ; saying with perfect patience to one of the most exacting, ' I had rather die, than fail a soul sent me by God '.

Such people show us what the common stuff of human nature can do, when abandoned without reserve to the action of God. They teach us, moreover, that Christian holiness is never monotonous. The household of faith is full of the variety and action, the ups and downs and temperamental surprises of real family life. There is room in it for artist and thinker, inventor and explorer, the nurse and the teacher and the simple useful woman, the mystic, the ascetic, and the practical man. Most of us, at one time or another, have been brought into contact with a saint of our own day ; and this experience, if we realized its nature, will almost certainly have seemed to us quite different from anything we had a right to expect. Looking back upon it, we see how baffled we were, and how entirely unselfconscious the saint was ; so simple, direct and disconcerting, with a certain sturdy spiritual realism, a happy childlike interest in small things, free from all taint of that professional piety which is sometimes mistaken for holiness. Sometimes, it is true, the saint may seem to us a solitary and almost terrible figure ; matured by sufferings and renunciations of which we hardly dare to think, and standing, like St. Simeon Stylites on his pillar, on the very summits of human nature, where the common life with its ceaseless stream of small events ceases to have meaning, and the unchanging God is all in all. But this is only one side of the truth about him ; and for Christians, perhaps, the least important side. That definition which describes the saint as doing all that others do, but for a different reason, brings him into focus ; and corrects the other-worldly emphasis. It reminds us that Christian holiness is always very human. It finds God in all things, as well as all things in God ; transforms, but does not abolish, personality. There is no such thing as a ' saintly type '. The psychological material which is transmuted by the Spirit is common to the race ; and retains to the end its deeply human characteristics.

The passionate desires, conflicts, weaknesses and rebellions, which are so frankly disclosed to us in the early lives of Jerome and Augustine, Francis of Assisi, Elizabeth of Hungary, Angela of Foligno, Ignatius Loyola, Catherine of Genoa and Teresa, are those with which our daily experience makes us only too familiar. So too their gifts of mind and temperament are those of the natural man. The massive personality of St. Bernard, together with his personal charm, the forcible character and brilliant mind of St. Hildegarde, would have given these people dominance in any walk of life. The humour and intelligence which led St. Teresa to ask for deliverance from ' silly devotions ' and Mother Janet Stuart to tell the ardent novice to pray for common sense, were a part of their natural endowment : and even the peculiar insight exhibited by St. Philip Neri, the Curé d'Ars, Huvelin and many others, was at least as much a psychic as a spiritual gift. It is not the possession of abnormal faculties, but the completeness of their abandonment to the over-ruling Spirit and consequent transformation of personality, which separates these men and women from ourselves.

It is true that the steady pressure of this Spirit compels the growing saint to die—sometimes with a drastic suddenness, as St. Paul; sometimes bit by bit, as St. Teresa,—to the restless, unreal, and self-occupied life of average men and women. But this is only in order to become a more wide-open channel of the Absolute Life; a serviceable weapon of the Divine creative will. Living with an intensity which entails for him the extremes of suffering and of joy, the saint is always, at his full development, both active and contemplative—as indeed every living member of the Mystical Body is bound in some manner to be—giving in devoted service that which he receives in child-like prayer. This must be so, since for the Christian saint, union with God means union with One who is both Here and There, both humble and Almighty, self-given and transcendent. Therefore it cannot mean mere flight from this world and its needs, or any other private satisfaction however spiritual and exalted. The very genius of Christianity is generosity, *Agape*; and the saint stands out as the self-emptied channel of that supernatural Love. The rich, active and life-giving character of Christian holiness depends directly on the Christian doctrine of the Nature of God. By that constant re-immersion in the atmosphere of Eternity which is the essence of his prayer, the Christian saint becomes able in his turn to radiate Eternity: and the more profound his contemplation, the more he loves the world and tries to serve it as the tool of the Divine creative love. Though his more obvious labours may be as homely as those of Santa Zita or Brother Lawrence, as apparently academic as those of St. Thomas Aquinas, he is a fountain of ghostly strength springing up to eternal life within the world. For he has become—and this is perhaps the most satisfactory of all our imperfect definitions—a 'pure capacity for God'.

When we turn from these thoughts and observe the saints as they appear in history, their courage, their untiring labours, their heroism and homeliness, their amazing conquests over circumstance, their bracing common sense and eager generous love; then we get a wonderful and even a disconcerting vision of those 'diversities of operations' in which St. Paul discerned the working of the same Spirit of Life. We find at the birth of every great spiritual movement, an awe-struck and surrendered personality, seized and used by a Power other than itself; subdued to a purpose which he or she does not understand, and imperatively called to a career or an action, which often seems to bear little relation to its vast religious or historic results. Nor is the saint's vocation a satisfaction of his 'natural' tastes. St. Paul, in defiance of his deepest prejudice, must obey the goad, capitulate to the unseen Victor, and set out 'in perils oft' to the conversion of the Graeco-Roman world. The Church which timidly welcomed that disconcerting convert, received in his person an influence which was to transform her own character and ultimately the history of mankind; and the bewildered soul chosen for this mighty office must take up a vocation he never fully apprehended, and go forth 'as poor to make many rich, and as a liar yet telling the truth'. St. Jerome and St. Augustine, clever, passionate and fastidious, not obviously informed by charity, are drawn inch by inch, as by some skilful angler, to the place in the scheme which they alone can fill. We see them both thirsting for God, and therefore accessible to God; long before they are aware of all that the drinking of this chalice must entail. St. Jerome sought in the desert the exclusive joys of a contemplative life, only to retreat with exasperated nerves from that over-peopled solitude, and the maddening intimacy of the professionally pious. Thus he found in the end, by devious paths, the life-work for which he was most fitted, and most needed; and gave the Latin Bible to the Western Church. No one who reads the *Confessions* can suppose that St. Augustine, with the soul of a mystic and the tastes of a don, enjoyed being an over-driven Bishop, worried by the Donatists, and by the ceaseless demands of administrative work. Yet here too the over-ruling Spirit achieves Its purpose; with small regard to Augustine's natural desires and apparent gifts. Brain and heart are subdued to the occasions of God, and the son of Monica and student of the Platonists becomes a Father of the Church.

Again, St. Benedict only wished to escape the uncongenial worldliness of Roman society, and find a retreat where he could 'make good men'; and there sprang from this desire the vast Order which was one of the chief instruments of European civilization. St. Gregory was dragged from contemplation, St. Cuthbert from his solitary prayer on the Farnes, and obliged to become rulers of the Church, and shepherds of souls.

When we come down to the early Middle Ages and look at those two remarkable figures of the twelfth century—the young French aristocrat, who sacrificed his rank, his wealth, his comfort and became St. Bernard, and the German child of genius who grew up in the cloister and became St. Hildegarde of Bingen—we again find ourselves in the presence of the ruthless transforming Power. Both of them were people of immense initiative, energy and intelligence; captured and dominated by the passion for Reality, for God. Bernard—a monastic reformer and a great ecclesiastical statesman, who left his mark on the Europe of his day and influenced Christian devotion for centuries after his death—was all this and did all this, as the sacramental expression of his interior communion with God: Who, he says, entered his soul in prayer 'living and full of energy', and sometimes transported that soul out of itself and gave it 'a clear vision of the Divine Majesty'. There is the real Bernard, telling us what the real Bernard loved. But though we may be sure from his spiritual writings that the life he desired for himself was one of silence and loving contemplation, he became as a matter of fact one of the busiest men of his day; and said that the whole object of mystical contemplation was to make men better shepherds of souls—in other words, to increase their spiritual efficiency. It might be worth while, alike for the placid pietist and for the hurried modern Christian, to think a little about this deliberate judgement of a great and active saint. So too St. Hildegarde, possessed by that vivid first-hand sense of God which she called the Living Light, might not keep it to herself; but was compelled against her own will to act under its commands, and tell the world what it revealed to her. Again, that vision of the Crucified which changed the whole life of St. Francis filled him, it is true, with an unconquerable certitude and love; but it also said 'Repair my Church', and Francis, who was not specially drawn to labours of this kind, obeyed. What St. Thomas Aquinas, whom we think of as a great intellectual, really felt about his own academic career can be guessed by those who compare the *Summa* with the Corpus Christi hymns and such fragments of his personal prayers as we possess. Mr. G. K. Chesterton has well said of him, that he was 'a philosopher in public and a mystic in private, like all sensible men'.

Sometimes the hidden power makes startling choices. It lays hands on Angela of Foligno, vain, soft and hypocritical; forces her to tread one by one the thirty-three steps of the Way of the Cross, gives to her astonished soul a series of mighty visions of the Being of God, and makes of her a transforming influence upon the lives of her countless disciples. It hides Julian of Norwich in the anchoress's cell; and gives her a revelation of which the searching beauty only becomes fully operative centuries after her unmarked death. It calls the marvellous girl, Catherine of Siena, from humble surroundings to change history, produce a masterpiece of Italian religious literature, and die before she is thirty-three: and beyond all this—her greatest title to our reverent admiration, and greatest proof of holiness—makes of her a saviour of sinners and 'Mother of thousands of souls'. A transforming energy from beyond the world seemed to pour out through her to those whose lives she touched, because of the intensity of her Godward life. She was a creative spiritual personality: one of the wicket gates through which God came to men, and men went out to God. This young fragile girl of the people, simply in virtue of her passion for God, transformed the lives of turbulent men of action and learned ecclesiastics, and forced the most arrogant sinners to penitence by the energy of her secret prayers; bearing their sins and carrying their sorrows, and at last dying exhausted yet full of joy. I think she is one of the greatest witnesses to the power of pure sanctity, the direct action of the Infinite through finite souls, which history contains.

Again, St. Teresa, of whom most people still think as a visionary, an ecstatic, and writer of mystical works, is revealed when we study her life as supremely a woman of action, who was first prepared and then driven by God to the reform of a great religious order, in the teeth of all difficulty and opposition: undertaking in middle-age, burdened by ill health, journeys and labours which might well have daunted the young and strong. Or, on the other hand, St. Vincent de Paul, that most practical saint—taken from the tending of sheep to lay the foundations of modern philanthropy and reform the clergy of France—is found when we investigate his life to be driven and supported by the same other-worldly love. All that he does and all that he bears, is the fruit of his secret union with God. Again, a young French widow is inexorably driven from shop to convent, and thence as a pioneer of education to heroic adventure in the New World: and thus Madame Marie Martin becomes the Venerable Marie of the Incarnation. The luxurious Parisian, De Rancé, is sent to the austerities of La Trappe, the fastidious aristocrat, Aloysius, to the revolting duties of the pest-house, Elizabeth Fry is brought from a quiet country house to Newgate gaol, Henry Martyn from a Cambridge common room to labour and die in the far East.

That selfsame Spirit 'dividing to every man as He wills', snatches at short notice a young Jesuit from his spiritual father, and sends Francis Xavier to his lifelong exile as Apostle of the Indies. It gives the humble cobbler, Jacob Boehme, a stupendous revelation of Reality; and reaches out through his spirit in another time and country to transform the soul of William Law. It takes a dull and unattractive peasant lad, makes of him the hardly-educated priest of an obscure French village, and gives to him a passion for redemption which draws to the confessional of the Curé d'Ars every troubled soul in France. It calls the Abbé Huvelin, a brilliant Hellenist, a man of subtle intellect and delicate sensibility, to do that same transforming work by the power of sheer holiness, in the obscurity of a small Parisian church: and sends his great pupil Foucauld to find in the Sahara a martyr's death. It draws Mary Slessor from the Scottish mill and Albert Schweitzer from the Professor's chair;

and sends them to the African jungle in the same 'royal service'. And in all these, and countless others, it is one secret spring of action that operates a diversity of gifts. Even George Herbert's poetry is far better understood by us when we think of that figure prostrate before the altar in the tiny church of Bemerton—symbol of a self-immolation to the purposes of Reality which every artist shares in some degree—while the parishioners waited for the door to be unlocked, and the new rector's induction to begin.

How, then, are we to regard this mysterious passion; and where are we to place it in our chart of the nature of man? for without it, that chart is incomplete. In its highest reaches it may be as rare as any other form of genius, and certainly costs more than most: but it never dies out of the world. Yet there is nothing in that world's life to account for the emergence of Holiness. It is inexplicable from the naturalistic standpoint: for it does not serve the biological purposes of the race, but wages relentless war upon those very instincts by which racial dominance is assured. The saints, differing from one another in glory, character and call, do not represent a special triumph of human evolution. They represent the capture and transformation of the creature by an other-worldly energy and love, which becomes ever more absolute in its demands upon life: subordinating to itself, though not necessarily exterminating, all other interests, activities and loves. What we see here is the growing correspondence of a created spirit with the Absolute Spirit, God: and because of this correspondence, this reception by the soul of the penetrating radiation of the Holy, its gradual and utter transfiguration. The present moment comes to every one fully charged with God. To respond to Him without flinching as He comes in that moment—there to touch and accept His Eternity, undeflected by self-will or self-love—this is sanctity. It is, of course, the Foundation of St. Ignatius translated into the terms of actual life: the end of Man is to praise, reverence and serve God our Lord. Hence the great importance of the saints for any deep and rich view of human nature: an importance which belongs to metaphysics at least as much as to psychology, and points beyond both to the mysterious relation of the spirit of man to the Spirit of God.

SPIRITUAL LIFE

'SPIRITUAL Life' is a very elastic phrase; which can either be made to mean the most hazy religiosity and most objectionable forms of uplift, or be limited to the most exclusive types of contemplation. Yet surely we should not mean by it any of these things, but something which for most of us is much more actual, more concrete; indeed, an essential constituent of all human life worthy of the name. I am not proposing to talk about mystics, or any one who has rare and peculiar religious experience: but simply about ourselves, normal people living the natural social and intellectual life of our time. If we know much about ourselves, I think we must agree that there is something in us which, in spite of all the efforts of a materialistic psychology, is not accounted for either by the requirements of natural life or those of social life; and which cannot altogether be brought within the boundaries of the intellectual and rational life. Though as it develops this 'something' will penetrate and deeply affect all these levels of our existence, we recognize that it is distinct from them. It is an element which is perhaps usually dormant; yet is sometimes able to give us strange joys, and sometimes strange discomforts. It points beyond our visible environment to something else; to a Reality which transcends the time-series, and yet to which we, because of the existence of this quality in us, are somehow akin.

By talking of 'spirit' or 'spiritual life'—terms more allusive than exact—we do not make these facts less mysterious. But we do make it possible to think about them, and consider what they must involve for our view of the nature of Reality; what light they cast on the nature of man; and finally how this quality which we call 'spiritual life' calls us, as spirits, to act. In other words, we are brought up against the three primary data of religion: God, the soul, and the relation between God and the soul. Those three points, I think, cover the main aspects of man's life as spirit. They become, as he grows in spiritual awareness and responsiveness, more and more actual to him, and more and more fully incorporated in his experience. And they are all three represented in the life of prayer; which, taken in the widest sense, is the peculiar spiritual activity of man. By prayer, of course, I do not merely mean primitive prayer—the clamour of the childish creature for help, relief or gifts from beyond—though this survives in us, as all our primitive and instinctive life still survives. I mean the developed prayer of the soul which has taken its Godward life, its link with the Eternal, seriously; has knocked and had a door opened on to a fresh range of experience. Such prayer as that is just as much a human fact as great achievement in music or poetry; and must be taken into account in estimating the possibilities of human life.

We begin then with this fact of something in us which points beyond physical life, however complete that physical life may be, and suggests—perhaps in most of us, very faintly and occasionally, but in some with a decisive authority—that somehow we are borderland creatures. As human beings, we stand between an order of things which we know very well, to which most of us are more or less adapted, and in which we can easily immerse ourselves; and another order, of which we do not know much, but which, if we respond to it and develop a certain suppleness in respect of it, can gradually become the most important factor in our lives. We might sum this up by saying that there is in us a fringe-region where human personality ceases to be merely natural, and takes up characteristics from another order; yet without losing concrete hold upon what we call natural life. It is in this fringe-region of our being that religion is born. It points to the fact that we need to be met and completed by an order of being, a Reality, that lies beyond us. We are in the making; and such significance as we have is the significance of a still unfinished thing.

Of course, in the pitter-patter of temporal existence it is very easy to lose all sense of this otherness and incompleteness of life; this mysterious quality in human nature. Attention, will and intelligence have all been trained in response to the physical; and turn most easily that way. We live too in a time of immense corporate self-consciousness. Modern literature, with its perpetual preoccupation with the details of our emotional and sexual relationships, reflects this. Universals, and our relation to universals, are neglected. Yet without some recognition of our relation to Reality, we are only half-human ; and if we are alert, we cannot entirely miss all consciousness of the presence and pressure of that Reality, that eternal order, however we may represent it to ourselves. The strange little golden intimations of beauty and holiness that flash up through life, however they come, do present a fundamental problem to us. Are these intimations of Reality in its most precious aspect, the faint beginnings of an experience, a development of life, towards which we can move ; or are they mere will-o'-the-wisps ? Shall we trust them and give them priority, or regard them with the curiosity that borders on contempt ?

In other words, is reality spiritual ? Is the only concrete reality God, as the mystics have always declared ? And is that richly real and living God present to and pressing upon His whole creation, especially His spiritual creation ; or is this merely a pious idea ? Are man's small spiritual experiences testimonies to a vast truth, which in its wholeness lies far beyond us, or not ? We have to choose between these alternatives ; and the choice will settle the character of our religion and philosophy, and will also colour the whole texture of existence, the way we do our daily jobs.

We assume that the first alternative is the true one ; that men are created spirits still in the making, and can experience a communion with that Living God,

Spirit of all spirits, who is the Reality of the universe. What we call our religious experiences, are genuine if fragmentary glimpses of this Divine Reality. That belief, of course, lies at the very heart of real Christian theism. In thinking about it, we are not moving off to some peculiar or specialized mystical religion; we are exploring the treasures of our common faith. And the first point that comes out of it for us, I think, is the distinctness and independence of God and of Eternal Life: as realities so wholly other than the natural order and the natural creature, that they must be given us from beyond ourselves. A great deal of modern Christianity, especially that type which is anxious to come to terms with theories of emergent evolution and other forms of immanentism, seems to me to be poisoned by a kind of spiritual self-sufficiency; which tends to blur this fundamental and humbling distinction between the creature and God, and between the natural and spiritual life. It perpetually suggests that all we have to do is to grow, develop, unpack our own spiritual suit-cases; that nothing need be given us or done to us from beyond.

Were the fullest possible development of his natural resources the real end of the being of man, this might be true enough. But all the giants of the spiritual life are penetrated through and through by the conviction that this is not the goal of human existence: that something must be given, or done to them, from the eternal world over-against us, without which man can never be complete. They feel, however variously they express it, that for us in our strange borderland situation there must be two orders, two levels of reality, two mingled lives, to both of which we are required to respond—the natural and the spiritual, nature and grace, life towards man and life towards God—and that the life of spirit of which we are capable must come to us, before we can go to it. It is surely the true instinct of religion which fills the liturgy with references to something which must be given or poured out on us. 'Pour down on us the continual dew of Thy blessing'—'Pour into our hearts such love towards Thee'—'Without Thee we are not able to please Thee.' All summed up in the wonderful prayer of St. Augustine: 'Give what Thou dost demand; and then, demand what Thou wilt.'

So I suppose, from the human point of view, a spiritual life is a life which is controlled by a gradually developing sense of the Eternal, of God and His transcendent reality; an increasing capacity for Him, so that our relation to God becomes the chief thing about us, exceeding and also conditioning our relationship with each other. So here the first and second points which we were to consider—what we mean by a spiritual life, and what a spiritual life involves for us—seem to melt into one other. Indeed, it is almost impossible to consider them separately. For, what it means for us is surely this: that we are meant, beyond the physical, to contribute to, indeed collaborate in, God's spiritual creation; to be the willing and vigorous tools and channels of His action in Time. That is the spiritual life of man at its fullest development, the life of all great personalities; saints, artists, explorers, servants of science. It is a life infinite in its variety of expression, but marked by a certain deep eternal quality, a disinterested zest for perfection, in all its temporal acts.

When we come to make the personal application of these ideas, this view of the relation of our fluid, half-made personalities to God, and ask how, as individuals, we are called to act—and that is the third of the questions with which we started—we see that just in so far as this view of human life is realistic, it lays on each of us a great and a distinct obligation. Though the life of the Spirit comes from God, the ocean of our being, *we* have to do something about it. Utter dependence on God must be balanced by courageous initiative. Each of us has a double relationship, and is required to develop a double correspondence. First with the Divine Creative Spirit who penetrates and supports our spirits ; and secondly with the universe of souls, which is enlaced with us in one vast web of being—whether our immediate neighbours of the Christian family who form with us part of the Mystical Body of Christ, or the more widespread corporation of all the children of God, of which this perhaps forms the nucleus.

For those who see life thus, sustained and fed by a present God, and who can say with St. Augustine ‘ I should not exist wert not Thou already with me ’, the idea of mere self-determination, self-expression as an end in itself, becomes ridiculous. Further than this, the notion of souls, persons, as separate ring-fenced units, is also seen to be impossible. In many ways that are perceptible, and many others so subtle as to be imperceptible, we penetrate and affect one another. The mysterious thing called influence points to our far-reaching power and responsibility, and the plastic character of the human self. Because of this plasticity, this inter-penetration of spirits, those who have developed their capacity for God, have learnt, as St. John of the Cross says, how to direct their wills vigorously towards Him, can and do become channels along which His life and power can secretly but genuinely transform some bit of life. Devotion by itself has little value, may even by itself be a form of self-indulgence, unless it issues in some costly and self-giving action of this kind. The spiritual life of any individual, therefore, has to be extended both vertically to God and horizontally to other souls; and the more it grows in both directions, the less merely individual and therefore the more truly personal it will be. It is, in the truest sense, in humanity that we grow by this incorporation of the spiritual and temporal, the deeps and the surface of life; getting more not less rich, various and supple in our living out of existence. Seen from the spiritual angle, Christian selves are simply parts of that vast organism the Church Invisible, which is called upon to incarnate the Divine Life in history, and bring eternity into time. Each one of us has his own place in this scheme, and each is required to fulfil a particular bit of that plan by which the human world is being slowly lifted God-ward, and the Kingdom of God is brought in. This double action—interior and ever-deepening communion with God, and because of it ever-widening, outgoing towards the world as tools and channels of God, the balanced life of faith and works, surrender and activity—must always involve a certain tension between the two movements. Nor, as St. Paul saw, should we expect the double movement to be produced quite perfectly in any one individual: not even in the saints. The body has many members, some of them a very funny shape, but each with their own job. The man of prayer and the man of action balance and complete one another. Every genuine vocation must play its part in this transformation in God of the whole complex life of man.

Men are the only created beings of which we have knowledge, who are aware of this call, this need of putting themselves in one way or another at the disposal of Creative Spirit; and this characteristic, even though it be only occasionally developed to the full in human nature, assures us that there is in that nature a certain kinship with God. So every human soul without exception, because of this its mysterious affinity with God, and yet its imperfect status, its unlikeness from God, is called to undertake a growth and a transformation; which shall make of it a channel of the Divine energy and will. Such a statement as this, of course, is not to be narrowed down and limited to that which we call the 'religious' life. On the contrary it affirms the religious character of all full life. For it means a kind of self-oblivious faithfulness in response to all the various demands of circumstance, the carrying through of everything to which one sets one's hand, which is rooted in a deep—though not necessarily emotional—loyalty to the interests of God. That conception expands our idea of the religious life far beyond the devotional life; till there is room in it for all the multiple activities of man in so far as they are prosecuted in, for, and with the Fact of all facts, God-Reality. I need not point out that for Christians the Incarnation—the entrance of God into History—and its extension in the Church bring together these two movements in the soul and in the human complex ; and start a vast process, to which every awakened soul which rises above self-interest has some contribution to make. As we become spiritually sensitive, and more alert in our response to experience, I think we sometimes get a glimpse of that deep creative action by which we are being brought into this new order of being, more and more transformed into the agents of spirit ; able to play our part in the great human undertaking of bringing the whole world nearer to the intention of God. We then perceive the friction of circumstance, the hard and soft of life, personal contacts and opportunities, love and pain and dreariness, to be penetrated and used by a Living Influence, which is making by this means both changes and positive additions to our human nature ; softening, deepening, enriching and moulding the raw material of temperament into something nearer the artist's design.

Next, let us look for a moment at Prayer, as the special reflection and expression of this relation of God and soul of which we have been thinking. Prayer is, if not the guarantee, at least a mighty witness to the reality of the spiritual life. If we were merely clever animals, had no kinship with God, we could not pray : no communion between Him and us would be possible. Prayer, in its three great forms of Worship, Communion and Intercession, is after all a purely spiritual activity ; an acknowledgement of the supreme reality and power of the spiritual life in man. As St. Thomas says, it is a 'marvellous intercourse between Infinite and finite, God and the soul'.

If the first term of the spiritual life is recognition in some way or other of the splendour and reality of God, the first mood of prayer—the ground from which all the rest must grow—is certainly worship, awe, adoration ; delight in that holy reality for its own sake. This truth has lately returned to the foreground of religious thought ; and there is little need to insist on it afresh. Religion, as von Hügel loved to say, *is* adoration ; man's humble acknowledgement of the Transcendent, the Fact of God—the awe-struck realism of the seraphs in Isaiah's vision—the meek and loving sense of mystery which enlarges the soul's horizon and puts us in our own place. Prayer, which is so much more a state and condition of soul than a distinct act, begins there ; in the lifting of the eyes of the little creature to the Living God, or perhaps to the symbol through which the Living God reveals Himself to the soul.

It is mainly because we are unaccustomed to a spiritual outlook which is centred on the infinite mystery of God and not merely on ourselves and our own needs and desires, that we so easily become confused by the changes and chances of experience. And for modern men, confronted as we all are by a swiftly changing physical and mental universe, sweeping away as it must many old symbolic constructions, but giving in their place a fresh and humbling sense of the height and depth and breadth of Creation and our own small place in it, it is surely imperative to establish and feed this adoring sense of the unchanging Reality of God. It is easy so long as the emphasis lies on us and our immediate interests to be baffled and depressed by a sense of our own futility. Our whole life may seem to be penned down to attending to the horrid little tea-shop in the valley; yet this and every other vocation is ennobled, if we find time each day to lift our eyes to the everlasting snows. I think we might make far greater efforts than we do, to get this adoring remembrance of the Reality of God, who alone gives our work significance, woven into our everyday lives. There is no more certain method of evicting pettiness, self-occupation and unrest ; those deadly enemies of the spiritual self.

It is within this penetrating sense of God Present yet Transcendent, which braces and humbles us both at once, that the second stage of prayer—a personal self-giving that culminates in a personal communion—emerges and grows. Here we have the personal response and relationship of the self to that God who has evoked our worship. Adoration, as it more deeply possesses us, inevitably leads on to self-offering : for every advance in prayer is really an advance in love. ' I ask not for thy gifts but for thyself ' says the Divine Voice to Thomas à Kempis. There is something in all of us which knows that to be true. True, because of the fact of human freedom; because human beings have the awful power of saying Yes or No to God and His purposes, linking up our separate actions with the great divine action, or pursuing a self-centred or earth-centred course. This is the heart of practical religion, and can be tested on the common stuff of our daily lives. It is this fact of freedom which makes Sacrifice, with its elements of personal cost and confident approach, and its completion in communion, the most perfect symbol of the soul's intimate and personal approach to God. If worship is the lifting up towards the Infinite of the eyes of faith, self-offering is the prayer of hope: the small and fugitive creature giving itself, its thoughts, deeds, desires in entire confidence to the mysterious purposes of Eternal Life. It is summed up in the great prayer of St. Ignatius: 'Take Lord, and receive!'

But as the realistic sense of God in Himself which is the basis of adoration leads on to a realistic personal relationship with Him in self-offering and communion: so from this self-offering and communion, there develops that full and massive type of prayer in which spiritual power is developed, and human creatures become fellow workers with the Spirit, tools and channels through which God's creative work is done. That is the life of Charity: the life of friendship with God, for which we were made. Growth in spiritual personality means growth in charity. And charity—energetic love of God, and of all men in God—operating in the world of prayer, is the live wire along which the Power of God, indwelling our finite spirits, can and does act on other souls and other things; rescuing, healing, giving support and light. That, of course, is real intercession; which is gravely misunderstood by us, if we think of it mainly in terms of asking God to grant particular needs and desires. Such secret intercessory prayer ought to penetrate and accompany all our active work, if it is really to be turned to the purposes of God. It is the supreme expression of the spiritual life on earth: moving from God to man, through us, because we have ceased to be self-centred units, but are woven into the great fabric of praying souls, the 'mystical body' through which the work of Christ on earth goes on being done. We talk about prayer thus by means of symbols; but as a matter of fact we cannot really rationalize it without impoverishing it. It leads us into the world of mystery where the Creative Spirit operates; in ways beyond and above all we can conceive, yet along paths which touch and can transform at every point our humble daily lives and activities. Thus prayer, as the heart of man's spiritual life—his Godward response and striving—is seen to be something which far exceeds devotional exercises; and is and must be present in all disinterested striving for Perfection, for Goodness, for Truth and Beauty, or for the betterment of the children of God. For it means the increasing dedication and possession of all our faculties by Him; the whole drive of our active will subdued to His design, penetrated by His Life and used for His ends.

And last, coming down to ourselves, how does all this work out in the ordinary Christian life? It works out, I think, as a gradual growth in the soul's adherence to God and co-operation with God, achieved by three chief means: 1. Discipline, mental, moral, and devotional. 2. Symbolic and sacramental acts. 3. Ever-renewed and ever more perfect dedication of the will; death to self. This point, of course, is incomparably the most important. The others have their chief meaning in the fact that they contribute to and support it.

Discipline. This includes the gradual training of our faculties to attend to God, by the regular practice of meditation and recollected vocal prayer. Also such moral drill as shall conduce to the conquest of the instinctive nature; the triumph of what traditional asceticism calls the 'superior faculties of the soul', or, in plain English, getting ourselves thoroughly in hand. At least, in the experience of most souls, this will involve a certain moderate amount of real asceticism, a painful effort to mortify faults of character, especially those which are ramifications of self-love, and a humble submission to some elementary education in devotional routine. Under this head we get an ordered rule of life, voluntary self-denials, and a careful detachment of the emotions from all overwhelming attractions which compete with God. Acceptance of the general methods and regulations of the Church also comes in here, as the first stage in that very essential process, the socializing and incorporation of the individual life of prayer; that it may find its place, and make its contribution to the total life of the Mystical Body of Christ. None of this is actual prayer; but all of it, in various degrees, must enter into the preparation of the self for prayer.

Next, *Symbolic Acts.* Even if we can dare to say that there is such a thing as an absolute, and purely spiritual communication of God with the soul (and such a mystically inclined theologian as von Hügel thought that we could not say this), such absolute communications are at best rare and unpredictable flashes; and even where they seem to us to happen, are confined to the highest ranges of spiritual experience. They could never form its substance; and it would be an intolerable arrogance on our part—a departure from creatureliness bringing its own punishment with it—if we planned our inner life on such lines. We are sense-conditioned, and must use the senses in our approach to God; accepting the humbling truth that His absolute being is unknowable, and can only be apprehended by us under symbols and incarnational veils. This of course is both Christianity and common sense. But as well as this, we have to acknowledge that the real nature of His work within the soul is also unknowable by us. When we enter the phase of suffering, this truth becomes specially clear. Only by its transforming action within the mental or volitional life, purifying, illuminating, stirring to fervour or compelling to sacrifice, can we recognize the creative working of God. And even these inward experiences and acts, vital as they are for us, are still only symbolic in their conveyance of God. Récéjac's celebrated definition of mysticism, as 'the tendency to approach the Absolute morally and by means of symbols', covers, when we properly understand it, the whole spiritual life of man; for the ground of the soul where His Spirit and our freedom meet, is beyond the reach of our direct perceptions. There is therefore no realistic religion for the human creature which is not expressed in symbolic acts. We cannot cut our world into two mutually exclusive parts and try to achieve the Infinite by a rejection of the finite. And when and if those more profound and really mystical depths of prayer are reached where we seem indeed to be subdued to a Presence and Action which has no image, and of which we can say nothing at all—when the eternal background has become the eternal environment and we are sunk in God—then that very sense of an entire passivity which accompanies the soul's deepest action, of being, as Jacopone says, 'drowned in the Divine Sea', is surely one more tribute to the part played by symbolism in the normal process of the spiritual life.

And last, the essence of that life, *Dedication of the Will.* This of course is the ever-deepening temper of all personal religion worthy of the name. In its first movement it constitutes conversion; in its achieved perfection it is the very substance of the unitive life of the saint. But between those two points there is much work to be done and much suffering to be borne, by those in whom this self-transcendence, this supernatural growth, is taking place. Because of the primary importance of God's over-ruling action, and yet also the great importance of the self's free and willing activity, there must be within any full spiritual life, at least until its final stages, a constant tension between effort and abandonment, loving communion and ethical struggle, illumination and purification, renunciation of the will and deliberate use of the will: as the natural and supernatural aspects of personality, both invaded and subdued to the divine purpose, come into play, and the Will of God for that soul is expressed in calls to concrete activity, or to inward abandonment. So too in the actual life of prayer we ought to expect, and practise in some degree, both the deliberate effort of intercession and the abandoned quiet of contemplation. And as the soul grows in suppleness under these alternating stimulations—these 'stirrings and touches of God', as the mystics so realistically call them—so its sense of the divine action, which is always there but not always recognized, becomes more distinct and individuated: until at last, in the full theopathetic life of the mystical saint, it becomes a perfectly responsive tool of the creative will. 'I live yet not I.' That of course is a real statement of experience, not a piece of piety: an experience which is reflected in the abnormal creative activities and spiritual power of the saints, from Paul of Tarsus to the Curé d'Ars.

And with this, I think, we reach the answer to the question with which we began: what exactly is the spiritual life? It is the life in which God and His eternal order have, more and more, their undivided sway; which is wholly turned to Him, devoted to Him, dependent on Him, and which at its term and commonly at the price of a long and costly struggle, makes the human creature a pure capacity for God. And as regards the actual prayer, the secret correspondence which accompanies this growth, this will tend mainly to fulfil itself along two paths: upwards to God in pure adoration—outward to the world in intercession. The interweaving of these two movements in the special way and degree in which they are developed by each soul, is the foundation of the spiritual life of man.

SOME IMPLICITS OF CHRISTIAN SOCIAL REFORM[1]

THERE is among Christian men and women, a growing sense of the need of making the social order in which we live less inconsistent with the Spirit of Christ than it is at the present time: solving some of its most acute problems, and our own daily and hourly problems too, not in a spirit of compromise, but as Christian logic requires them to be solved. This is one of the most difficult of all tasks; for it means nothing less than the carrying through of the implicits of the spiritual world into every detail of the common life, bringing to bear on that recalcitrant common life the power and love given to us by our faith. And we must learn to look with humility, and also with intelligence—for this too is a gift of the Holy Ghost—at this supremely difficult thing, in order to learn how to set about it; for we have no doubt now that we must set about it,

[1] Address delivered at the Inter-Denominational Summer School of Social Services, held at Swanwick, to consider 'A Christian Order of Society', July 1922.

if our present confusions and miseries are to be healed. We cannot walk down a street of any of our larger towns without meeting the challenge of Christ.

Christian men and women. That means to us, of course, not what Jacob Boehme used to call 'mere historical new men' but living members of the mystical fellowship of the living Christ; members as it were of the great secret society of the universe, pledged to perfectly concrete and practical obligations, to the conscious furthering of the purposes of God. Conscious members too of that supernatural fellowship, which St. John declares to be the primary fact of the Christian life. 'Truly our fellowship is with the Father and with His Son . . . if we walk in the light, as He is in the light, we have fellowship one with another.' Fellowship here of course does not mean merely companionship; but utmost communion, oneness. Those who have experienced something of this reality, and surrendered themselves, at least in will and intention, to all that it demands, can hardly regard themselves in any other light than partners with Christ in the great and continual business of bringing the world of time into ever closer harmony with the eternal love and perfection of God.

The poet Donne said of Christ, in his sonnet on the Resurrection,

> 'He was all gold when He lay down, but rose
> All tincture'—

He was using the language of the alchemists; whose final aim was to make, not merely gold, but a tincture that should transmute into gold all the baser metals that it touched. In this phrase he seems to have caught and expressed the Christian secret: that the living Christ is a tincture, not added to life but transmuting life wherever He enters it; and therefore that we must seek to bring under that influence, not only the souls of individuals, but the corporate soul too, and so effect its transmutation. It is this change, not the imposition of a new moral code, which we should mean by the Christianization of society; for Christian law can only be understood and practised by Christian souls. Such a Christianization of society involves, ultimately, the complete interpenetration of God and human life; the drenching of life, on all its levels, with the Divine Charity—its complete irradiation by the spirit of goodness, beauty and love. This is fellowship with God: and nothing less than this ideal is fully Christian, because nothing less than this fully works out the incarnational idea, and gives all life its opportunity of reaching life's best levels in Christ. To say that this is impossible, is to say that Spirit cannot triumph; and so to deny the very foundations of our faith.

We turn from thoughts of this kind, and look round at the intricate and many-graded life of this planet, still holding tight to the conception of that life in its wholeness, as material for the working out of the incarnational idea: material of which the dominant character is, that it can be so used—so entinctured by the Divine Reason, Christ—as to make of it a graded revelation of God. Look particularly at the bit of life for which we are plainly responsible: the order of so-called Christian civilized society. That, supremely, is the material for the working out of the Incarnation to its full term. It was confided to us. Here we are, or can be, the actual tools through which the Divine Wisdom works out His purpose of perfection. Real Christianity, real consecration, means becoming such a tool.

There is a celebrated chapter in the *Visions and Revelations* of that great mystic and spiritual teacher Angela of Foligno, which tells how soon after her conversion, as she was walking alone through the vineyards between Spello and Assisi, she heard the Holy Spirit saying to her, wheresoever she looked, ' Behold and see ! this is My Creation '. And, gazing on that exquisite landscape, bathed as it is in the light which we see in Perugino's pictures—a light which seems to be the veil of a more spiritual loveliness—she was filled with an ineffable sweetness and joy. And then all her sins and errors came back into her mind, and she was possessed by a humility such as she had never known before. We can translate that scene for ourselves, thinking of such a spring as that which we had this year : the beauty of the untouched English country, snowy with hawthorn, the downs starred with tiny perfect flowers, the amazing emerald life of the young beechwoods, the exultant singing of the birds—and the Spirit of God saying still in our hearts ' Behold and see ! this is My Creation ! ' We too, seeing this living and intricate beauty, were surely filled with gratitude and delight.

But now, reverse this picture ; and suppose that we are condemned to go with Christ to some of the places which we, in our corporate capacity—Christian citizens of a Christian country—have made, or allowed through stupidity and sloth to come into existence. Imagine any one of us walking through the East End of London, or up the staircase of a lodging-house in Notting Dale—and then through Piccadilly, and up some staircases which one could find near there—or down our prison corridors—or through a poison-gas factory—with that Companion at our side. And suppose that it is our turn to meet that glance and say 'Behold and see! This is *our* creation'. We can each complete that episode; but none without shame. Even to think of the contrast is surely to be possessed in our turn by such a penitence as we have never known before.

If we dare to complete the episode, to turn from this monumental exhibition of our corporate failure in intelligence and love, our greed, apathy, stupidity, lack of energetic faith, and look at the face of Christ; then, we cannot feel any doubt about the nature of the command which is laid on us. We have to meet that vision, fair and square,—that infinite love and compassion which ought to be our love and compassion too—with the knowledge in our minds that there are places in all our great cities where it is not possible for a child to grow up in unsullied purity. This is our creation. We know what Jesus thinks about children; and He brings to us the mind of God. Again, complete classes of the population are kept in a state of economic insecurity, which thwarts for them all chance of spiritual development: and we must hold such spiritual development—by which I do not mean piety—to be God's will for all men. There is a level of deprivation and anxiety, just as there is a level of luxury, at which the soul's life cannot prosper; where animal interests and anxieties alone can survive. This poverty is not holy and simple, but sordid and degrading; and this is our creation too. It makes stunted, diseased, imperfect, wasted lives; ugliness, bitterness and tension. The soul's inherent beauty and possibility are taken and twisted out of shape, by our worse than animal acquisitiveness, our steady self-occupation and indifference to the common good.

Christ demands the surrender of acquisitiveness: and ultimately a social order in which we can say to all men and women without irony, in respect of their bodily necessities, 'Your heavenly Father knoweth that ye have need of all these things: but seek ye first the kingdom of God and His righteousness and all these things shall be added unto you'. That alone—the corporate security which comes from the practical application of neighbourly love—is Christian citizenship. I do not say that this means the triumph of any particular *ism*: but it does mean, plainly, a triumph of the love and generosity of God in the heart and mind and strength of every individual of which that social order is built. Energy and intelligence, as well as mere feeling, dedicated to the purposes of Christ; and then brought to bear on the desperate problems of our corporate life. We have got that corporate life into such a mess now by our persistent acquiescence in a policy of clutch, that its problems seem to present insuperable difficulties; but there are no insuperable difficulties to Divine Love. It is strange that any Christian should look upon such a notion as fantastic, since it is merely the corollary of our faith in the power and present work of the Holy Spirit within life. Because of this faith we do not look upon it as fantastic, and do look upon the social order which neglect of Christian realism has brought into being, as grotesque. Therefore we are bound to consider, in a spirit of prayer and with an entire willingness to pay the necessary price, how best to tackle some of the problems which have been brought into being by this triumph of acquisitiveness over love.

This involves a preliminary problem, to be faced by each of us: how to acquire, and to hold, that attitude of mind and heart which shall make us the most efficient tools of the Spirit of Christ, keep us in a measure—as He was supremely—at one and the same time hidden in God, yet wholly dedicated to His unstinted service, the furthering of His aim in our fellow-men. We shall only be useful in this work in so far as we achieve this; speaking and acting as men and women of prayer, whose souls are opened wide towards the world of spirit, and have received its penetrating gift of energy and peace. We must have the habit of recourse to Eternity and its values; must respond directly to God quite as often, and in as real, devoted, and intimate a spirit of love and service, as we respond to our fellow-men. He is the one Reality, the one Touchstone: His revelation in Christ the Pattern from which we must never depart, bringing to it every practical question and difficulty. Professor Lethaby in a recent book on town planning, appealed for the fostering in men and women—and specially in children—of the sense of the sacredness of their town: of its comeliness, dignity, beauty, as the outward expressions of the corporate soul, something which all could love and seek to further and preserve. Did we have this, we should come to feel that hideous buildings, vulgar advertisements, and still more bad and degraded housing conditions, were actual insults offered to the Spirit of God; and we should try perhaps instead to do honour to His holy power in our constructive work, considering all its problems in that Universal Spirit, to which George Fox was always inviting us to have recourse. But this means a firm grasp of the fact of God's Presence, a perpetual keeping of the Pattern in focus; and this is not to be had unless we pay attention to it.

In the *Yearly Meeting Epistle* of the Society of Friends for 1920, the question was asked: How can we gain a new spirit? How can we break loose from our fears and suspicions and from the grip of complacent materialism, and face the issues with new faith in God and man? And the answer is: Only by a fresh sense of the presence and character of God. I am convinced that this is the right answer, and the key to success in the work which we want to do. In the long run 'we behold that which we are' say the mystics 'and are that which we behold.' Our outward lives inevitably come to harmonize with our real ideals; our vision of truth depends upon truth within. As our hearts are, so do our aim and our treasure come to be. This is true of society as well as of individual souls; the corporate life of a people that beholds the Eternal Beauty will tend to be beautiful in its turn. Psychology is insisting more and more on the importance of that which it calls the Imagined End ; the need of placing before our inner vision a clear picture of that which we want to achieve. This imagined end acts as a magnet, drawing and unifying our will, energy and desire. Whether our aim be health, success, or holiness, the same principle applies ; we tend towards that which we clearly envisage as possible, and really desire. In this enterprise then it is above all things necessary that we should give ourselves a chance of looking at the end —the Kingdom, the realization of the Love of God—that we should constantly look, watch, listen, for the intimations of eternity : and judge by this majestic standard the sins and omissions, the cheap expedients and selfish negligences, which enter into our dealings with the temporal environment within which our wills operate. Be still, and know ; in order that you may be. Realize the superb possibilities of your material, the august power of creation that has been put into your hands ; and do not conceive life in terms of jerry-built villas with garage attached. Look at your pattern, instead of working by rule of thumb. Seek spiritual food, and give yourselves time to assimilate it ; so that you may be strong. Before we can mend our unreal confusions, we must have a clear vision of the Real : and the gaining and holding of such a vision in personal life is one of the main functions of prayer, as in corporate life its holding up is the chief business of institutional religion. Efforts to Christianize our social conduct are foredoomed, unless those who undertake them give themselves time to look steadily at Christ.

Beyond this vision of the pattern, perpetually

blurred, perpetually to be renewed if we would be true to it, there is also the question of power. Christianity is a religion of power; and if it were not so, our undertaking would be hopeless. Recourse in prayer to the Unchanging and Eternal is recourse to the very sources of our life. The saying in the Fourth Gospel, 'I am come that they might have life, and have it more abundantly', is a practical, not merely a devotional, statement. *Zoe*, the 'more abundant life' offered to every real Christian, is not anything vague or metaphysical. It means, in modern jargon, a real enhancement of our life-force; that mysterious vital energy of which the Spirit of God is declared to be Lord and Giver, and which conditions our body and mind, showing itself in our power of dealing with circumstances. This is an absolutely practical promise; making a sharp division between the person who only believes in Christianity, and the person who experiences it. Christian regeneration is not only a supernatural but also a psychological fact, which enhances efficiency, feeds power, gives life; and it does this by the sublimation of our vigorous instinctive nature, its unification and total dedication to one end. It does really initiate a series of changes in us—often slow and painful—which can bring us in the end, if we do not shirk them, into perfect and life-giving harmony with the Will of God.

Therefore we bring to our study of the Christian social order and how we can work for it, this principle: that only by constantly looking at the Pattern can we keep ourselves trued up for this job, and only by recourse to supernatural sources of power can we get the strength to put it through. History proves this to us. It shows us, again and again, that men and women of prayer tap a source of energy, possess a tranquil courage, an initiative, a faith, entirely unknown to those who have not set up and deliberately maintained through thick and thin these willed and loving contacts with the Eternal Life in which we 'live and move and have our being'. And it warns us most solemnly that, entering—as I believe we are entering,—on one of man's recurrent efforts to actualize the Spirit of Christ, we defeat our own purpose, cut ourselves off from the true fountain of that more abundant life which we shall need for it, unless we so order our existence that the life towards God keeps pace with the life lived for our fellow-men.

There is in William Blake's 'Jerusalem' a marvellous drawing of the pitiful and energizing Spirit of Christ brooding over Albion ; stretching His wounded hands to those two limits which Blake calls Adam and Satan —all the possibilities of our humanity (for Christ is, after all, the Son of man) and all the worst we have become. It seems to me we too are bound to strive for such a spiritual gesture ; the stretching out as it were of one hand towards His perfection, the limit where Divine and human meet, and of the other, in complete friendliness and generosity, towards the sins and imperfections of men. Neither action is particularly easy in a practical way ; but unless we try to manage this, we need not regard ourselves as genuine friends of Christ. It is the double, simultaneous outstretching that matters ; this only can open the heart wide enough to let in God, and so make of each man who achieves it a mediator of His reality to other men. The non-religious socialist seems to stretch out one hand, and the non-social pietist the other. But one without the other is useless. Both at once : that is where the difficulty comes in. It sometimes seems a demand which we can hardly meet.

Mediators of God's reality to other men : this is to be in our small way workers with Christ. It means the constant interpretation to us of God's thought and will by the living Spirit, known to us in the life of prayer, and its constant handing on by ourselves, in the active life of human intercourse and service. It means the translation of unchanging Perfection—the pure reality of Eternal Life—into human terms : such concrete human terms as national, civic, industrial, family relationships. It means this actualization of God ; given to us spiritually, in all that we mean by the contemplative side of life, and laying on us the obligation of expressing it on the practical side of life. Never one without the other. Not the life of devotion divorced from the effort to bring in, here-and-now, the Kingdom of God ; not, most certainly, the hopeless effort to actualize the Kingdom without the life of prayer. We want to bring the creative spirit of Love —perpetually offered to us but never forced on us—to bear on the actual stuff of human life ; and for this, we must make strong and close contacts with both orders, the spiritual and the human worlds.

St. Teresa said that to give our Lord a perfect service, Martha and Mary must combine. The modern tendency is to turn from the attitude and the work of Mary ; and even call it—as I have heard it called by busy social Christians,—a form of spiritual selfishness. Thousands of devoted men and women to-day believe that the really good part is to keep busy, and give themselves no time to take what is offered to those who abide quietly with Christ ; because there seem such a lot of urgent jobs for Martha to do. The result of this can only be a maiming of their human nature, exhaustion, loss of depth and of vision ; and it is seen in the vagueness and ineffectuality of a great deal of the work that is done for God. It means a total surrender to the busy click-click of the life of succession ; nowhere, in the end, more deadly than in the religious sphere. I insist on this because I feel, more and more, the danger in which we stand of developing a lop-sided Christianity ; so concentrated on service, and on this-world obligations, as to forget the need of constant willed and quiet contact with that other world, wherefrom the sanctions of service and the power in which to do it proceed. For those who are seeking to solve the problems of citizenship in a Christian light, that willed contact is of primary importance ; so too is the inward discipline, the exacting, personal, secret effort and response, to which we shall find it impels us. Do you suppose that we can, so to speak, hop into our uniforms, let enthusiasm avail for efficiency, and win the battle thus ? Most certainly not. We all believe now in education for citizenship ; training for social service. Far more should we believe in training for spiritual service, for participation in the building of the City of God ; and this has not much in common with what commonly passes for religious education. It means in practice the effort to live some sort of inner life harmonious with the great principles of Christian spirituality; penitence, renunciation, self-surrender, and daily recourse to the peace and power of God.

Here, then, those who desire to work most fruitfully for the Kingdom have a most delicate discrimination to make. Because plainly it is not Christian to concentrate too much attention upon one's own soul; yet on the other hand, our own inward growth does condition both our communion with God and our power of helping other men. We see this double strain in all great religious teachers, and in all the best helpers of humanity. It is exhibited on a grand scale in St. Paul, St. Augustine, St. Francis, St. Teresa, Fox, Wesley; in all of whom an unremitting, intense inner effort, an exacting life of self-discipline and prayer, an alert sensitiveness to the Presence of God, kept pace with outward deeds. Remember Elizabeth Fry, balancing her marvellous regenerative work by silent worship. Remember General Booth travailing in spirit, and creating the Salvation Army. The breezy modern doctrine which we so often hear recommended—go straight ahead, fill your life to the brim with service, and your soul will take care of itself—this notion receives no support whatever from the real heroes of practical Christianity. They were keenly aware of their own disharmonies and inward conflicts; and felt these to be a source of weakness, as they are. They knew they must resolve these conflicts, if the Holy Spirit was to work through them without impediment, if they were to grow, and achieve the stature in which they could best do the work of Christ. So in them, penitence kept pace with love, and prayer with work. Conscious loving dependence on greater sources of power—fellowship with God—was the cause of their success: and the fact that our Lord's own teaching and works of power and mercy appear closely dependent on the nights which He spent on the mountain in prayer, might make us hesitate about abandoning this, the classic norm of Christian life. The effort towards Christian citizenship, in fact, must begin by the effort to be, ourselves, each one of us, citizens of the City of God.

The English mystic, Walter Hilton, has a beautiful and celebrated passage in which he describes pilgrim man travelling in desire towards that City: how he sees it on a hill, small and far away, yet real, as a pilgrim first sees Jerusalem. It seems to him at that distance very tiny, hardly more than a rood in length; nevertheless he knows it to be no mere vision, but the true home of his soul. When he reaches it, he finds it is within 'both long and large, that without was so little to his sight' a very roomy place, full of every kind of dwelling, a home for all manner of men: and he discovers that this city he has been journeying towards so long is nothing else but that concrete Love of God to which the soul attains when it ascends the Mount of Contemplation. And Hilton ends his parable thus: 'This city betokeneth the perfect love of God, set in the hill of contemplation; the which, to the sight of a soul that without the feeling of it travelleth towards it in desire, seemeth somewhat, but it seemeth but a little thing, no more than a rood, that is six cubits and a palm of length. By six cubits are understood the perfection of a man's work;

and by the palm, a little touch of contemplation . . . nevertheless, if he may come within the city of contemplation, then seeth he much more than he saw first.'

Consider this well; for here we have a formula, by which to true up our own conceptions of citizenship in the Kingdom of God. It demands two things: 'the perfection of a man's work, and a little touch of contemplation'. That means the union of skill and vision, both consecrated. One without the other is no good; we shall not get the measurement of the city right. Accept then this conception of the Kingdom of God on earth, as built up by man's very best work, directed by man's very best prayer; and see what it must mean in efficiency and beauty, industry and joy. Take that measurement into slums, factories, schools, committee rooms, labour exchanges and building-estates—the perfection of man's work and a little touch of contemplation—and then, measure against this scale ourselves and our average performances. The first result will probably be profound humiliation. We shall perceive ourselves, face to face with the social muddle, incapable of that perfection of work which its rebuilding requires: and of the sharp vision of the Pattern on the hill, which will give us faith in the possibility of actualizing it on earth, in a Christian order of society. It is a long way off, hardly in focus yet; nevertheless, let us at least travel towards it, as Hilton asks us, in thought and desire.

With this thought in our minds, of the perfect union of work and of prayer demanded of us by Christ, if His purpose is to be fulfilled by His friends, look at the programme for this week. It points out to us three great forms of social wrongness, which inhibit the free action of God's will for men: our acquiescence first in materialism, next in the principle of conflict, and last in social and racial injustice. Where the love of God declared in Christ alone should rule, if we mean anything by Christianity, these three things rule instead. If we look more closely, we see what they represent. Not so much man's wilful wrongness—though each offers opportunity and encouragement to all his lowest and most unloving impulses—but rather a failure to push forward; a relapse into those lower levels of life from which God, as we believe, is drawing out the human soul into His own light. They represent the natural tendency of man to camp in the marshes, instead of undertaking the climb upwards to Jerusalem: his failure, as psychology would say, to sublimate and adapt to new levels the crude forms of that instinct of self-preservation which once under other conditions served him well. They show that our impulsive minds, which really control our actions, are still the impulsive minds of primitive men; ruled by fear and anger, pride and possessiveness, unredeemed by the Perfect Man revealed in Jesus.

Our materialism is the survival and accentuation of primitive man's necessary preoccupation with the material world; the immense importance for him,—if he were to survive at all—of food, shelter, possessions; the sense that they are valuable for their own sakes, and being won with difficulty, must be clutched tight as the very substance of his life. Our spirit of conflict, whether shown in industrial competition or international struggles, represents the survival of that pugnative instinct which impelled the primitive, in a world full of inimical forces, to fight for his own hand, his own family, his own tribe. Our class and racial antagonisms represent the wrong development of that herd-instinct which was perhaps one of the very first instruments of man's social education ; teaching him his first lessons in brotherhood, obedience, self-subordination to the common good, but also tending to assemble him in exclusive groups which are smaller than his capacity for love.

These antique tendencies, immensely strong, are now so cunningly disguised and rationalized that very few of us realize the half-savage and half-childish nature of the impelling instinct which causes us to love a bargain, to collect things for collecting's sake, to judge rich and poor by different standards, to resent a trespass, blindly to support our own class or country, to enjoy combative games and destructive sports, to feel uplifted by a patriotic song. None of these impelling instincts are wrong in themselves ; but they are now occasions of wrong, because we have failed to sublimate them. We let them go on, in altered conditions, giving us suggestions appropriate to the Stone Age ; instead of harnessing these vigorous springs of psychic energy to the chariot of Christ. To do this (1) We must replace material by spiritual values—the respect for wealth by the respect for beauty, the desire for goods by the desire for good, the desire for luxury by the desire for justice ; quantity by quality ; must dissolve acquisitiveness in that spirit of poverty which enjoys everything because it desires nothing. (2) We must replace the belief in achievement through conflict and the defeat of our adversary—whether in the international, the economic or the political field—by belief in achievement through love, united effort, and the winning of our adversary: 'Loving the unlovely into loveableness.' (3) We must replace tyranny between class and race by love between class and race; fraternity, the true fulfilment of the herd instinct, overflowing its first narrow boundaries till it embraces the world.

But these are mental and spiritual imperatives; they spring up from within, they are not imposed from without. They remind us again that the Christian order of society can only come into being as the expression of a corporate Christian soul. If we want to produce it, we must first produce a corporate change of heart; bit by bit Christianizing the social body from within, so that it may become more and more incapable of acts that conflict with the principle of love, and of tolerating for others conditions which we would never allow to affect those individuals for whom we really care. Corporate regeneration must follow the same course as personal regeneration. Accepting, like the individual Christian, the Incarnation as the clue to life, the community must grow into conformity with this belief. It can only do this along the same lines as the individual; namely, by a balanced process of analysis and synthesis. It must first track down and realize the true springs of its conduct; press back into the racial past, and discover the humiliating facts about those impulses which really condition our behaviour in such matters as nationalism, property, employment, servitude, sex. It must acknowledge how many notions necessary to a primitive state of society have become imbedded in our view of life; and, thanks to the conservative nature of the social mind, still govern our corporate view of existence. It must further realize that these relics of the past, however imposing the disguises they now wear in financial and political circles, represent something less than man's best here and now possibility: and that therefore our wholesale capitulation to them, our quiet assumption that you cannot go against 'human nature' in its most acquisitive, self-regarding, and combative mood, has the character of sin. Having reached this level of self-knowledge, it may perhaps be brought to something equivalent to social penitence: may feel as a direct reproach every life damaged by bad housing, every child maimed by economic conditions, every soul stifled by luxury or obsessed by unreal values, every man or woman embittered and made hopeless by unemployment and friendlessness. And then, turning in one way or another to God, to Reality, to the true values declared in Christ, the work of whose creative Spirit its mingled stupidity and selfishness retards, society may set in hand the complementary movement of synthesis: the real building-up of Jerusalem, by perfect work and steady prayer.

Let us take, as a last thought, a picture from current philosophy: that great vision of the so-called new realists, of a universe which has, as they say, a *tendency to deity*, is moving perpetually towards the actualization of God. That picture, for Christians, indeed for all truly religious minds, must be incomplete. Yet does it not represent, as far as it goes, a real view of the Holy Spirit dwelling within our world of change and ever seeking more perfect incarnation in life? And is it not man's supreme vocation to co-operate in this? Consciously to forward the creative aim of Divine Love; take his share in the business of the spiritual world, which is lifting all things up into the order of Divine Reality. These may seem very metaphysical, possibly even unreal, considerations, to put side by side with our pressing problems of internationalism, economics, family life. But philosophy reminds us again, that unless we can set the particular details of our actual life within some such universal background, we shall never understand their significance; and that a first duty of thought is to get this universal background right. At present the universals within which we see our particular social order are wrong, because not Christian; hence the wrong interpretation is put upon particular facts, and a wrong scale of values obtains. Our need, then, is the re-birth of our vast potential energies into a world of fresh values, in which each particular action would be given the meaning that it has for the Mind of Christ. It is an exacting standard, but we dare not aim at less: for we cannot forget that for Christians human nature, human love, and human life, find their controlling law and their perfect fulfilment on Calvary, and not on any lower level than that. But to remember this, to keep our eye fixed on it, means living in the spirit of prayer: and to live up to it means an unremitting effort, both social and individual, to Christianize our every action through and through, and so fulfil the destiny of our souls.

THE WILL OF THE VOICE[1]

IN Bernard Shaw's great prophetic play *Back to Methuselah* Eve, the Mother of humanity, says in her old age of her grandson Enoch: 'Enoch walks on the hills and hears the Voice continually, and has given up his will to do the Will of the Voice . . . but it took Enoch 200 years to learn to interpret the Will of the Voice.' That may seem a strange quotation to bring to the opening meeting of a great Conference which represents to those who have convened it a moment full of promise in the history of British Christianity. But we are here because the Churches and Christian bodies that we represent are all committed, like Enoch, to the walk with God, and want to learn to interpret the Will of the Voice. We are the delegates of men and women of all types who agree in refusing the animal view of existence: who desire to know God's nature and conform to His purpose—to live, that is, towards the standards of Divine Reality. We want a clue to the thread of God's purpose running through this tangled creation; and we want it all the more because we are so solidly sure about Him. We feel that, so far, we have neither

[1] Address delivered at the First Session of the Copec Conference, Birmingham, April 1924.

interpreted nor obeyed the Voice. We have been not so much wicked, as stupid, muddled and vague.

Yet when we take humanity as a whole, when we think of its lowly origins, what marvellous insights we have been given into God's eternal character and purpose; into the superhuman facts of holiness and of love! Put all this together—the best and deepest that we have known—the whole Christian inheritance of spiritual truth and beauty—all the witness of the saints—all they reveal of the realities of that spiritual world towards which we stretch out in our little prayers. Put together these inconceivable disclosures of God—'fairest yet strongest, unchangeable yet changing all'—given to us, little half-animal things. Add to them the ultimate disclosure, made actually, by the most humbling of condescensions, in human nature itself: and then confront all this with the use that we have made of it.

Consider again, that as Christians we do actually possess the clue to God's Will which we ask for. We are allowed to perceive in Jesus Christ the inmost nature of God, and His relation with the world, in the degree in which our little human souls can bear it. We have seen the emergence in human history of perfect holiness and ceaselessly redeeming love, as solid facts. We could, as the saints have always done, live with His continuing Spirit here and now, if we were willing to pay the price. We can, in our prayer, touch infinite and hardly guessed forces, draw on an unfailing source of power; the living water of Creative Love. In other words, the nature and purpose of the Infinite God are, and always have been, doubly revealed to us: in the facts of history, and in the spiritual contacts of our own inner life. And in the life and teaching of Our Lord these two channels of revelation in their fullness come together: in His Person the life of history and the life of prayer met, and the result was the vision of the Kingdom of God, the assigned end at once of social and of individual growth. Look at that vision, and then look at this planet, of which we are the responsible inhabitants. It is needless to say more about that.

Now, is it not our task, is it not the solution of our problem—open as we are to both these great currents of reality—to bring together and harmonize the life revealed in history and the life revealed in prayer? Are we not here, really, as delegates from Christian bodies whose right to exist depends on knowing and proclaiming this? Is not the whole of the New Testament a demand that this shall be done? Does it not declare that there is a power accessible to us, in which it *can* be done? When we think of the perpetual miracles of personal redemption worked by the supernatural grace of God, can we dare to say that the wider miracle of social redemption is beyond the Christian span? Surely we cannot venture to limit the influence and possible transfiguring power of God upon the history which He pervades, sways, yet transcends. This very conference has come into being as a result of the pressure of God upon history. It is a part—we don't know what part—of His great mysterious and unceasing action on human thought and human life. All limitations to that action are ours, and are the very essence of our sin. It is our frightened selfish resistance, or, worse than our resistance, our disgusting pious apathy, our dull certainty that social regeneration won't happen, which stops it from happening. Our frightful lack of the dynamic virtues—Faith, Hope, Charity. In one of the deepest declarations of the New Testament, the very object of the Incarnation is described as the bringing into humanity of a more abundant life : which we might perhaps translate as the bringing into the stream of history and social life of that other stream of supernatural energy—that vivid grace—which feeds the individual soul. Do we seem to have appropriated that energy ? Are Christians in the bulk so vividly alive ? Has something been added to their power, as well as their obligation ?

A genuine Christian ought to be alive all over, with a depth and vitality of soul that makes shallow judgements and prejudices impossible. A Christian social order should be permeated in every part by this life ; controlled by a supernatural aim. If it were so, how full that order would be of joy and of vigour, how transfused by adoration and love ! But it isn't, is it ? What we seem to have done, on the contrary, is to make life on the natural level a failure, and on the supernatural level an impossibility, for all but a mere handful of souls. What about all this ? Have we, with our wonderful access to the hills, with our Christian vision and Christian privileges, yet failed in our common life to interpret the will of the Voice ?

Remember, we claim to know. Every member of the Conference is the delegate of a society that believes it is trying to follow Jesus Christ; that accepts Jesus Christ as revealing the real character of the Infinite God, the nature of Reality, the conditions of fellowship under which alone we can be truly real. It is quite easy to denounce such statements as idealism. But they are not. They are realism; and what is wrong with current Christianity is that it does not face all the implications of that fact. Hence its vision and prayer have been divorced from its action; and thus both sides of its life have been maimed. We have forgotten the second thing that Enoch did. He gave up his own will, in order to do the will of the Voice; and that means unconditional consecration.

Christianity was given to us as a complete revelation in human terms of God and His purpose, demanding from us a completeness of surrender and response. But we have snipped it at both edges, limited both its supernatural and its natural outlook, and made it ineffective and incomplete. We have reduced its supernatural vividness and splendour, its holy beauty, its hardness and romance. We have lost our instinct for Eternal Life. And having done that we find, as we might have expected, that this sterilized Christianity is strangely impotent upon the natural plane. So the purpose of this Conference and the prayers of those who have called it together will never be fulfilled by the mere passing of resolutions, or the framing of rules and principles which Christians can apply to the problems of active life. It will only be fulfilled if the Church again becomes a Church of Prophecy and Vision; and like Enoch, in that which some choose to call her old age, listens to the Voice and learns to interpret its will. She must follow her Master to those nights upon the mountain from which He returned with power to teach and heal the world, if she would restore to full vividness the completely integrated Christian life of adoration and of action, and so remake the bridge between the natural and supernatural worlds—lifting the life of human intercourse in all its phases to the level on which it ought to be, the level of sacrament.

As it is, whilst we are talking theology, or going to church, or sewing the miserable little patches we call charity and social service into the rotten garment of our corporate life, or perhaps are enjoying those tiny apprehensions of God to which we can attain, in what we childishly believe to be a 'spiritual' way—whilst we are indulging in these various religious pursuits, I had almost said religious amusements, countless human souls as dear to God as our own are passing through this world under conditions of which no Christian, no lover of Christ, with an ounce of imagination, can bear to think; conditions which make their achievement of full spiritual life impossible. Thousands of us are eating what we suppose to be the Bread of Eternal Life at our brothers' expense. We cannot seriously suppose that this represents the purpose of God, the will of the Voice. Yet we continue our devotional basking in the sun, our religious self-cultivation; and let the maiming influence of environment play on these myriads of other souls, pressing them back to the animal levels. We just don't give them a chance.

The mystics, with their deep experimental sense of

God, and of all that is involved in His service, had a hard name for this kind of thing. They called it 'adorning Christ's Head, and neglecting His Feet'. 'Surely', says one, 'He will more thank thee and reward thee for the meek washing of His feet when they be very foul, and yield an ill savour to thee, than for all the curious painting and fair dressing thou canst make about His head by thy devout remembrances.' 'His feet, ragged and rent'—ragged and rent with treading roads we have made so much rougher than they ought to be. Yet those feet are as much a part of His mystical body as the superior cells which see and interpret the world's beauty and truth; and unless our outflowing love and reverence goes equally and actively to *all* parts of His incarnate revelation, can we hope to read His purposes right?

The mystic Ruysbroeck says that the Love of God enters the little but uplifted soul of man as a simple light: and then it grows, and becomes a spreading light, which flows out to all in common. Now the infinite and all-creative Love of God comes into the soul of the Church in the simple light of Christ. But it has not there been transformed into the spreading light which shall redeem the whole world; it has not been fully used, fully applied. And the result is that even in the Churches, which are created to foster it, the light somehow seems to burn rather dim. Has the simple light given to us in the story of the Magdalen been generally applied to human sin? or that of the Good Samaritan to the obligations of brotherhood? or that of the Pharisee and Publican to moral and religious values? As to the Sermon on the Mount, it is really a series of indictments, is it not, of our 'wonderful modern civilization'; so absolutely clear of all suspicion of poverty of spirit, purity of heart, mercy, meekness, peace! It is needless to continue: we know quite well that our country is not a Christian one. In other words, we know that the bit of this planet for which we are responsible is not corresponding with God's nature or fulfilling His purpose. And we have let the confusion get so dense now, that we can't cut our way out of the thicket; we can only proceed bit by bit to the restoration of Faith, of Hope, of Charity.

I began by quoting one modern prophet; now I will quote another. In a recent essay, Bertrand Russell pointed out the frightful danger involved in the modern alliance between man's half-savage impulses and his growing scientific power; and having done this, he said, 'Only kindliness can save the world; and even if we knew how to produce kindliness we should not do so, unless we were already kindly'. Now I do not propose to do as far too many apostles of social Christianity have done; reduce the pure Love of God to organized kindliness. But no one can deny that living, vivid, realistic Christianity—the reign of Christ's Love in individual hearts—*does* make men kindly and more than kindly. It lights the fire of supernatural charity, compassion, self-sacrifice. It turns the prose of humanitarian conduct into poetry, turns a decent attitude to our fellows into love. And if one of our most distinguished and least theological minds, trying every path, has discovered that only love in its various kinds and degrees can put the world right—what is this, but a demand for the widespread application of the Christian secret; another indication that man is growing, and beginning after many errors to interpret the Will of the Voice? 'If we knew how to produce kindliness, we should not do so unless we were already kindly.' That is a word of deep wisdom: for the Christian attitude and action are only produced and appreciated by implicitly Christian souls—that is, those whose vision of God transcends their vision of themselves and their own interests. Real kindliness, in our little half-real and dimly-conscious spirits, can only emerge as the faint reflection of a Love that immeasurably exceeds and precedes our own.

If we believe that the Incarnation reveals to us the character and purpose of the Absolute Love; then it becomes a great illumination of the mind, as well as a stimulus to our love and will. It links our struggle, all, every bit of it—the falling sparrow, the child, the worker, the deliberate and redemptive suffering and renunciation of the clear-sighted and pure—all this it links with God's achieved Perfection, with a Power and Spirit that will be more and more operative in us, the more fully we give ourselves to their work and ends. 'All things work together for good to them that love God!' If they don't for us, perhaps this may have something to do with the quality of our love. The love of God demands courage and industry. It must be whole-hearted, without a hint of reserve. No dread of awkward consequences. No mean hankerings after safety and comfort. 'Not worn out with labours, not daunted with any difficulties!'

The love of God that is truly operative, is the total self-giving of our tiny wills to His will; nothing, however hard, that is really demanded held back in the name of prudence or reasonable behaviour. Only that personal unlimited surrender can help us, I am convinced, to interpret the Will of the Voice; to see the proportion in which our tiny notions of necessity stand to His Nature and Purpose.

I read the other day the story of a Brownie who lived in a wood.[1] He had a little wheelbarrow and passed his time in a very moral and useful manner, picking up slugs and snails. Yet there was something lacking in his life. The King of the World passed through that wood very early every morning, and made all things beautiful and new; but the Brownie had never seen Him—he longed to, but something prevented it. He had one cherished possession; a lovely little soft green blanket which had once fallen out of the fairy queen's chariot, and which he hadn't been able to help keeping for himself. It was very cold in the wood at night, but the blanket kept him so warm and cosy, that he never woke up in time to see the King of the World. And one day there came to him a Shepherd, who looked deep into the soul of the Brownie, and said to him 'Haven't you yet seen the King of the World?' And the Brownie said 'No. I do so want to, but somehow I can't manage it.' Then the Shepherd replied 'But I seem to see something in your soul that keeps you from the Vision; something that looks rather like a blanket!' And at that a terrible fight began in the heart of the

[1] *Visions in Fairyland,* by D. Sewell.

little Brownie—a battle between wanting to go on being warm and comfortable in his blanket, and the longing to see the King of the World. Perhaps the ultimate choice which lies before us may turn out to be the Brownie's choice between the Heavenly Vision and the Blanket.

THE CHRISTIAN BASIS OF SOCIAL ACTION[1]

THERE is a strange little story in the early annals of the Franciscan Order, of how Brother Giles, one of the holiest of the first Companions of Francis, deeply shocked some Dominican friars by the casual observation that St. John the Divine really says nothing at all about God. In answer to their horrified exclamations at this apparently profane utterance, Brother Giles went on to say that one might think of God as a mountain of grain, as great as the Monte Cetano which was towering above them; and of St. John as no more than a sparrow, who picked here and there a few odd grains from that unmeasured richness, without making any real impression upon it at all. In which it appears to me that St. John proved himself to be indeed the patron saint of all theologians.

It was with this searching little story in my mind that I read the terms of reference which are put before this Summer School, namely: 'To discover and to define the Catholic doctrinal basis for the Christian life, personal and social.' We are further told that we are successively to study from this point of view

[1] Paper read at the Anglo-Catholic Summer School, Oxford; 20 July 1925.

the World-order, the Nation, the Industrial order, and the Home ; and in the course of our explorations shall have to consider three things :

(*a*) The implications of the Catholic faith in practical life.

(*b*) The distinctive Catholic principles on which social action should be based.

(*c*) The view that the manifold activities of life when rightly understood all come within the range of religion ; and constitute a unity in God which theology must express.

Considering these statements over against the mysterious Presence of God, I then began to wonder which among the particular grains of truth which mankind has brought home from the mountain were to be regarded as 'specific Catholic doctrines'. It sometimes seems to me that the distinction between Catholic and non-Catholic is not a very fruitful one : and that the distinction between those who do, and those who do not, love and adore God revealed in Christ and refer all things to Him, goes deeper into the reality of things. But if we keep to the language of our syllabus, and try to define the essence of Catholic Christianity, I suppose the first things that come to mind are the Catholic emphasis on the Incarnation and its continuance in the sacraments, and the concept of the absolute value and authority of the Church as the Mystical Body of Christ.

When, however, we look further, these doctrines are seen to derive their deepest significance from the fact that they are special demonstrations and developments of one over-ruling truth ; which we might call the priority of the Supernatural, and its presence and revelation in and through the natural. Catholicism requires the central truth of God as Spirit and Father of Spirits, the one Absolute Reality; and of this God-Spirit, as eternal, loving, personal, prevenient and self-revealed—supremely in what we call the Incarnation, continuously in various degrees in the sacraments of religion and of life. If we accept this philosophic position, our first proposition will then be that Catholic doctrine is uncompromisingly theocentric. For it, in the last resort, only God matters. And this at once means that the Catholic can never consent to *mere* social and material betterment, as being in itself a sufficient Christian ideal. We are called to seek perfection—all kinds of perfection—only because God is perfect first. So if we wish to discuss our first term of reference—the Catholic doctrinal basis of the Christian life—we must look first at the Catholic idea of God and the soul's relation to Him. Of course the real virtue and the doctrinal heart of any religion always is decided by its idea of God; and Christian effort in the past has often failed through forgetfulness of this. And it is that richly living concept of God's concrete reality and utter distinctness from the world, yet His ceaseless activity within and for every bit of it, escaping monism on the one hand and deism on the other, which is decisive for Catholicism. We must balance that deep, awed sense of the transcendent mystery of the mountain which alone is truly religious, by the certitude that even the sparrow can and must go there for its food.

This position means that the Catholic attitude

towards existence can never be merely naturalistic or this-world. It can never permit religion to become merely an aid to the full and virtuous living out of the natural life. It fixes the mind, not on the possible perfecting of the animal creation, but on the ever-growing and never-finished perfecting of the spiritual creation. It must refuse to attribute absolute value to the world of change, save in so far as it incarnates the Unchanging. It requires a constant sense of mystery, depth, the supernatural ; it is, in fact, a two-step religion.

Again, Catholic philosophy can never regard as complete any theory of the spiritual life based on self-development from within ; nor can it consent to the doctrine of the soul as an impenetrable monad, or expound the possibilities, apprehensions and experiences of that soul on the basis of ' unpacking its own portmanteau, and explaining itself to itself '. Everywhere in life, though in varying degrees, it requires and finds the prevenient presence and action of something other than Nature : the vivid reality of grace, Spirit, God. Thus it rests on a profound duality, which goes right through religious experience, and must govern our view of personal and social life : the distinctness and over-againstness of the eternal and the historical, of God and the soul, of grace and nature.

Yet, on the other hand, Catholicism emphatically declares an intimate contact between all these pairs of opposites. Spiritual reality is not and never can be cut off from the world of sense. There is at every point a penetration by God of the world : a truth which of course underlies the doctrine of the Holy Spirit. Hence the God of Supernature is also the God of Nature; and it is not Christian to say that the *world* is very evil, although *we* often are. Christianity says that the Father of the Eternal Wisdom is the father of the sparrow too.

This emphasis on the over-ruling reality and distinctness of the supernatural, yet refusal to make water-tight compartments between it and the natural, covers, I think, all the affirmations most distinctive of Catholicism: the Incarnation considered both as a general truth and as historical fact, sacramentalism, the Communion of Saints. It commits the Catholic at least to a modified dualism. It commits us to the view that the spiritual life of humanity is not completely articulated unless it has an inside and an outside too: and that in so far as we are aware of spiritual values, we are bound to try to give them adequate expression in the world of sense. It rejects mere unbridled immanence on the one hand, and a sharp separation between God and the sense-world on the other hand. It recognizes that matter and sense do play their part in all contacts between God and the soul; and that therefore the phenomenal world has and retains true importance, even in the loftiest reaches of spirituality. And here it provides a point of departure for discovering the method and aim of Christian social action. Such a view is consistent with the general trend of the great New Testament writers. Indeed, the first clause of the Lord's Prayer at once commits us to the view that we are creatures of supernatural affinities; that our real status cannot be understood merely as a development from within the natural order, for this only tells half the truth about the soul. And the whole of the spiritual life can be regarded as a progressive realization of this truth, as we expand into fuller personal being ; deeper, humbler and more loving awareness of God. From one point of view all real human progress means such spiritualization—in technical language, a growth in and a yielding to grace—and the practices of religion are the food and helps of this growth.

If then we regard man's life, corporate and individual, from this angle, where shall we stop ? Where are the frontiers of human life and possibility to be fixed ? And how shall we reconcile such a thorough-going other-worldliness with our obvious this-world obligations ? This is a problem which ought to be before the minds of all social reformers. As Catholic Christians they cannot logically acquiesce in any schemes for the making of a social order, however otherwise desirable, that shall oppose or check in any way the trend and expansion of the soul's supernatural energy. They can never accept the Utopia of the kind-hearted materialist ; or give comfort, safety, even political freedom, the rank of a Christian ideal. Civilization and spiritualization are not the same thing ; and for the Christian, spiritualization must always come first. On the other hand, we are bound to work for the elimination, here and now, of all conditions hostile to that spiritualization ; all checks on the soul's healthy life. Thus the many things which are plainly hostile—drink, prostitution, bad housing, tyranny, reduced moral standards, embittered class or race relationships—become of intense importance, even, and perhaps specially, to the most thorough-going supernaturalist ; and are all matters with which religion ought to deal.

But we cannot stop there. Such a general view of the intimate relation of the natural and spiritual is not sufficient unless it is regarded as the preparation and incentive of action. The recognition that God acts within life by means of the material order brings with it, or should bring, a further recognition that we in our turn are called upon to be the creative instruments of God in space and time ; co-operating according to our measure in the ceaseless loving action of His Spirit upon life. The sparrow in whose beak a grain of the living manna has been placed, is therefore bound in its strength to do his best for the sparrow world. True, religion will deal best with the problem of evil by its own method of individual inward sanctification, which was the method of Christ. But such personal sanctification is the first of two movements. It is only in the exceptional and purely contemplative nature that the obligation to incarnate God's Will, further the redemptive action of the Holy Spirit, can be met by devotional self-expression alone ; and even in such natures, the more purely the flame of contemplation burns, the more in the end it is found to inspire saving action. This proposition could be illustrated again and again from the lives of the Saints. We cannot sit down and be devotional, while acquiescing in conditions which make it impossible for other souls even to obey the moral law. For it is not God who imposes such an impossibility. It is we, in the corporate sense, who do so; and we have no right to ask God to mend conditions, unless we are willing to be ourselves the tools with which the work is done.

The obligation to do something about this seems to me to rest with crushing weight on every Christian communicant, for reasons which are too sacred to be given detailed discussion here. But at least we can say that there must be a sense in which the whole world and everything in it is sacred to us because God loves it; and therefore we are committed to doing our best in, with and for it—our best physically and mentally, as well as our best spiritually. I should like to see the Ignatian act of consecration recited after all those prayers in which we ask the Divine Love to do something about the social and industrial miseries our Christian civilization has produced: 'Take, Lord, and receive all *my* liberty; *my* memory, *my* understanding, *my* will, all *I* have and possess.'

There are, I suppose, two main ways of taking religion. The religious soul may withdraw more and more from the world and the life of the senses, in order to go by the path of negation to God. Or it may merge itself by love and surrender in the creative Will of God; and in and with that Will, go out towards the whole world. This, of course, is the way of Christianity. Thus we arrive by another path at the conclusion already stated: that the God of the natural and of the supernatural is one, and therefore, though physical and spiritual must ever be distinguished, they must never be put into opposite camps, for this rends the Body of Christ. The rushing out of Christ's love and admiration towards flowers, birds, children, all the simple joyous unspoilt creations of God, was part of the same movement, the same passionate desire to further the glory of God in His creatures, which showed itself in acts of healing, compassion, and forgiveness towards disease and sin ; and in anger and indignation towards selfishness, meanness and hypocrisy. All these were various exhibitions of the perfect harmony of His soul with the Spirit that loves and upholds the world.

Thus adoration can never exempt the Christian from this-world action ; and this-world action, however beneficial, will fail of effect if its foundations are not based upon the life of adoration. To go back to Brother Giles's parable, the sparrow must go to the mountain ; but it must also live the common sparrow life, build its nest, and feed its young. The awed sense of the mystery in which we live, and which enfolds and penetrates us, must not stultify our small human activities, but improve them. It is by this alternation of the transcendent and the homely, the interaction of lofty thought and concrete thing—all the friction and effort consequent on our two-levelled human life—that the true growth of human personality is achieved.

We put all this in more philosophic language when we say that being a Christian, loving God, 'finding and feeling the Infinite', does not absolve us from being part of history ; or from a full entrance into, and dealing with, the life of succession. On the contrary, it commits us to the task of trying to work out God's purpose in history. Even the contemplative vocation is entirely misunderstood by us, if we suppose its essence to consist in a solitary and purely spiritual relationship to God. It is, in its fullest expansion, a special arduous and sacrificial method of dealing with the sins and discords of life. The duty towards which any incarnational philosophy points us is the bringing forth within historical succession of more and more of that abiding power, the 'something insusceptible of change', which transcends history. The true life and wonder of the human soul consists in its power of embracing and combining both these terms: the fact that it is able to be intimately concerned both with being and with becoming. And the same is, or should be, true of the corporate soul of society.

Now since what philosophy calls the 'absolute values' are statements about the character of God, though of course incomplete statements—grains picked by the sparrow off the mountain—it is plainly a part of this ability and duty of the soul to try to incarnate these absolute values within that order, that world of succession, with which we are able to deal. The Parable of the Talents hints that the common practice of giving them decent burial in consecrated ground, instead of taking the risks involved in putting them out to interest, is not in accordance with the vigour and realism of the Mind of Christ. St. Augustine's 'My life shall be a real life, being wholly full of Thee' sums up, from this point of view, the Catholic standard both of individual and social action. We must desire this deeper realness not for ourselves only, but for all men, and for all those institutions in which men are combined—since we are called to love all other souls as much as our own, and God above all souls—and must oppose and try to eliminate all that conflicts with such expansion of personality. The doctrinal basis for Christian action then becomes the obligation to make the world of life such that it can be wholly full of God ; that His Kingdom may come and His Will be done, unimpeded by anything which we can rectify, as fully within the historical order as in the eternal scene. For the real theme alike of Catholic philosophy and Catholic sacramentalism is the continuing intimate presence of God in history ; and His revelation through historical processes, historical persons, sensuous symbols and impressions. The bold Athanasian epigram 'He became human that we might become divine' at least warns us against any inhuman aloofness from the natural world. That natural world, that historical order can never of course be adequate to Him ; but are nevertheless destined, according to their measure, to incarnate His life and convey it. Anything which contributes to this end has a right to our support and sympathy. Anything which blocks the way to it we must regard as an evil, and as the proper object of Christian attack.

Thus, in refusing to do our best to improve and purify the social order, we are refusing the religious obligation to make it so far as we can a fit vehicle of the Spirit of God. Redemption is bound to have its this-world aspect ; and it is perhaps its this-world aspect which is specially committed to our care. Hurried transcendentalists do well to ponder the extent in which our Lord's short ministry was concerned with the homely details of man's life. 'I have felt ', said John Woolman the Quaker, ' a longing in my mind that people might come into cleanness of spirit, cleanness of person, cleanness about their houses and gardens ; and I think even the minds of people are in some degree hindered from the pure operation of the Holy Spirit, where they breathe much of the bad air of towns.'

Here Woolman is surely in line with the homely and human spirituality of the New Testament, and its perpetual acknowledgement of the close interdependence of body and soul, of inward and outward things. Indeed, if the Creator be also the Father, and creates and redeems by and through a physical order, that physical order, once we really understand it, must turn out to be a thing of infinite importance and possibility. And the way to understand it is to love it. ' God so loved the world ' involves a totally different theology from ' God so loved the souls in the world '. If, with Baron von Hügel, we agree that the human spirit is called to ' a humble creaturely imitation of the Eternal Spaceless Creator, under the deliberately accepted conditions, and doubly refracting media, of time and space ', then this must involve in our own small way something of His loving, all-merciful, generous dealing with all the needs and problems of the world.

The first article of the Creed—I believe in God, Father Almighty, Maker of Heaven and Earth—really contains within itself the full Christian obligation to deal with social problems. If the Eternal Creator be indeed a Father caring even for the sparrows, this lays on us the duty of loving interest in all He cares for and sustains. The wider the circle of this love and interest of ours, the nearer it comes to embracing *all* created life—the more perfect, in other words, our Charity—the nearer we are to the ideal set before man in Christ. The reality of the ascent of our spirits in communion and prayer can best be tested by the extent in which they 'flow out in love to all in common'. The intensity, and special field of action, of this outflowing interest will vary in individuals. But it is a function of the Body of Christ in which all are concerned.

If we accept these principles, then the real problem before us falls into two parts. First, what we ought to do, and why; secondly, what our ultimate objective ought to be.

What we ought to do, and why. We ought always to work for the elimination of any conditions which we could not tolerate for persons whom we love; and which, on a higher plane, we see to be inconsistent with our best ideas of God. The reason why we ought to do this is because, for the Catholic Christian, the sacramental principle is operative over the whole range of life, in countless ways and degrees, and he is obliged to hold that God comes to man through and in natural means. We must therefore improve those natural means in every department of experience. And we are bound to be personally active in this matter because our own sanctification is only the first of two movements; and is chiefly important as making us instruments with which the Spirit of God, indwelling history, does His work.

What our objective ought to be. The objective of the

Christian supernaturalist must surely be a material world which shall further in every possible way, for all men and at all levels, the life of the soul ; a natural order which shall be the matter of a sacrament expressing the supernatural. This does not mean the necessary elimination of pain, tension, difficulty, hard work, or temptation. It means seeking to make these, for all men, more and more contributory to the growth of spiritual personality, instead of hostile to it. Such a programme has nothing whatever in common with an ideal of general comfortableness. Christian conduct can never be actuated merely by humanitarian considerations. On the contrary, it seems to me that the Catholic sociologist must at least try to achieve a balance between the ascetic and the benevolent outlook and action : the balance which we see so perfectly achieved in Christ. Ascetic as regards man's spiritual growth and purification ; benevolent as regards his natural status and rights. Christian social reform is not merely the effort of a number of clever, kindhearted, well-intentioned animals to make things as pleasant and wholesome all round as they possibly can. So far as it is a genuine activity of the spirit, it is the response of our individual spirits to the pressure of God's creative love, our effort to let that love find ever fuller expression through our action—one of the ways in which the Eternal Wisdom uses human personality 'as a man uses his own hand'. We do not bring to it a true sense of vocation until we feel this ; and feel, too, that all in it which truly matters points beyond this world.

What do those searching and terrific sayings of

Christ—perhaps the most terrific of all His utterances, when we realize their full implications—about the giving of a cup of cold water, the meat given or refused to the hungry, the receiving of the little child, really mean? What in fact, is involved for us in the one saying which He makes decisive for the ultimate destiny of the soul?

'Inasmuch as ye have done it unto the least of these My brethren, ye have done it unto Me.'

Surely there is something here far deeper and more drastic than a general invitation to 'good works'; or the sentimentalisms of a certain type of pious philanthropy? Does not this bring us once more, from another point of departure, to a practical acknowledgement of the universal, intimate presence of the Divine life in history: an extension of the Incarnation which does not stop short of our humblest experiences, and which means that our attitudes and acts towards our fellows are always in this sense attitudes and acts towards God? This discovery of the Eternal God in other men—in every grade and aspect of natural life—does not mean pantheism. But surely it does mean loving, and doing all we can for these His lowly dwelling-places and manifestations among us; purifying and unselfing all human relationships. It means too that we cannot dare to claim the benefits of His self-identification with our interests, unless we in our turn are ready to identify ourselves with the interests of other men; not merely those interests we choose to call moral and religious, but every difficulty, longing and need. When Angela of Foligno, at her supreme moment of apprehension, exclaimed 'The whole world is *full* of God!' did not this vision embrace a whole multitude of paths, those we call physical as well as those we call spiritual, along which God flows in on man, and may and will be reached and served by us, so long as we truly mean and intend Him? Such a view involves the possible consecration of every material act. Placed within this living and personal conception of the Divine Immanence, 'Inasmuch as ye have done it—' takes on fresh depth and almost unbearable poignancy. It means the discovery, within social contacts of every kind, of an opportunity for the direct service of Eternal Love; and this must involve far more than a mere unorganized kindliness. It means approaching the problems of social life with our heads as well as our hearts; remembering that it is within our power to make social science a department of theology. The apocryphal saying of Christ 'Blessed art thou O Man if thou *knowest* that which thou dost do!' is supremely true of those who achieve this: and marks the difference between the Christian social action which begins at the altar and comes back to the altar, and the merely ethical sort.

Now what have we said? Really this: that the ultimate doctrinal basis of Christian personal life and social action is that rich conception of God, as both transcendent to and immanent in His world, which it is the very business of Catholic worship to express in its intensest form. And further, that this conception of God, when it becomes to us a living, all-penetrating reality and not a theological statement, is found to require from us a life which spends itself in love and service on this world, whilst ever in its best expressions and aspirations, pointing beyond it. A life, in fact, moving towards a goal where work and prayer become one thing; since in both the human instrument is completely surrendered to the creative purposes of God, and seeks more and more to incarnate the Eternal. Since what is true of us one by one must surely as we rise into a fuller humanity become true of us in groups, we have here a principle which might at last become operative in our international, political and civic relationships. As corporate Christians we cannot be satisfied with a merely individual application of our faith. We must set as our goal such an expansion—through, in and with us—of creative and redeeming love, as shall embrace the whole world and be operative on every level of our many graded life.

What would the acceptance of such principles mean ? It would mean that every Christian must work for a social order in which the outward would become ever more and more the true sacramental expression of the inward. And as an essential preliminary to this, much faithful purification of that outward; the disharmonies, atavisms, sterile passions and disguised self-seekings which the individual Christian is obliged to face and conquer on his way towards union with God, must also be identified and conquered by the group. Penitence has its social aspect; there, too, humanity is surely called upon to recognize a wrongness that can become a rightness, and the need of action as an earnest of contrition.

But the social order which should emerge from such a realistic correspondence with Reality would not be distinguished by a tiresome uniformity, or any oppressive and Puritanical goodiness. It would possess a rich and inexhaustible variety in unity; for it is called to reflect a facet of the Mind of that God Who loves children as well as students, and has created tomtits as well as saints. It would be a social order in which energy would not be wasted in mere conflict; in which every talent and vocation had its chance. It would give a great place to the contribution which those who seek truth and beauty make to our knowledge of God. It would recognize this world as a theatre of the spirit. Whilst acknowledging and encouraging all innocent and legitimate fields of action, it would yet leave room for, and point to, a life beyond the world; giving fullest opportunity for the growth of those spiritual personalities in whom eternal values are incarnated, and through and by whom Holiness is glimpsed by us. A world-order in fact obedient to the God of Supernature and of Nature; and permitting the fullest development, interplay and mutual support of the active and contemplative lives. For this and only this perpetuates within history the full and balanced Christian ideal. Only this permits man to incarnate according to his measure—and even under the simplest, most homely accidents—the Eternal in human life. Thus he feeds upon and makes his own those few small grains he brings back from the mountain: whilst yet recognizing and adoring, beyond the possible span of all these, his little discoveries and realizations, the unmeasured and unsearchable richness of God.

THE IDEALS OF THE MINISTRY OF WOMEN[1]

WE shall all feel it undesirable that the last speaker at such a Conference as this should introduce any controversial note. But I feel bound in honesty to state in a few words my own position in regard to the main issue, before I go on. I am opposed to the giving of the priesthood to women; for many reasons, and chiefly because I feel that so complete a break with Catholic tradition cannot be made save by the consent of a united Christendom. Any local or national Church which makes it will drop at once to the level of an eccentric sect. On the other hand, I greatly desire and also expect an immense extension and recognition of women's ministry in other directions than this. Properly 'rooted and grounded' in lives of real simplicity and self-abandonment, this must conduce to the well-being and enriching of the Church's life. Hence the great importance for the future of a right conception of our situation; what we have to give, and how we can give it best. But these, after all, are merely the views of one insignificant individual looking out on

[1] Paper read at a Conference called by the Central Council for Women's Church Work, October 1932.

the external situation; and any individual view of that external situation, how it should and how it may develop, is mostly guesswork at the best. We do not want to end there, but rather by reminding ourselves once more of those realities on which anything pleasing to God in our work must depend. If we are true to those realities and seek to increase our hold upon them, then surely, whatever our status as workers for the Church and whatever recognition we may or may not get, we shall be able to be useful to Him and to souls. And that, and that alone, is the point.

What, after all, *is* Christian ministry, male or female, lay or ecclesiastical? It is, or should be, just the attempt of some one who cares supremely about God to cherish and help in one way or another the souls that are loved by God: to be as one that serveth. And moreover it is an attempt that is made, not because we feel like it or choose it, but because we are decisively pressed, called, put to it. 'You have not chosen me, but I have chosen you'. The word vocation does not mean that we do the calling. It is true, alas, that we often seem to see this principle ignored; but is it worth while to consider the sort and degree of pastoral work which we *might* do, unless we are prepared to do everything which comes our way from that centre? 'Lovest thou me? Feed my sheep.' That is the real point, isn't it? and the only one. Over against that, all discussions about our call and status, and what we ought to be allowed to do, and what we have to contribute, and whether the shepherds accept us as trained shepherdesses, or more often regard us as auxiliary dogs—all that fades into silence.

That real teaching saint, Father Benson of Cowley, said: 'It is a sign of perfection to be willing to do anything'; yes, even under the orders of the curate you don't much like. Supple, equal to any burden and any job, because the burden of one's own importance has been given up. Surely a body of women aiming at that type of perfection would do more for God than a body of women who had achieved some particular status. The work that endures, and that is worth while, comes always from an immense self-surrender; and only that kind of ministry is going to increase the power and vitality of the Church. It really is not worth our while to struggle for the opportunity of giving anything less than that. No kind of assertiveness whatsoever can serve the purpose of the supernatural life. That merely blocks the Divine right of way; prevents the Spirit from getting through. If it is true—and I think perhaps it is true—that the movement of that Spirit within the Church is opening fresh paths along which women can serve God and souls; then how careful we must all be, to balance our initiative and devotedness by great patience, suppleness, and self-oblivion. We surely cannot wish to give up the sacred privilege of the lowest place.

Here we must try to avoid doctrinaire conclusions which arise from disguised self-will, and be entirely at the disposal of God. Do you remember the beautiful story of the Vision of Pier Pettignano? He saw the Church Visible as a superb procession following after Christ on the Way of the Cross, all the ecclesiastics, dignitaries, and officials each in their place and each with their credentials. And at the end of it all came the shabby little figure of St. Francis, in his patched tunic; with no credentials, no position, drawn only by love. And he alone was walking in the very footsteps of the Crucified.

I have known a few women in my life who have genuinely ministered to souls in a creative way: who truly gave the living water and the heavenly food. They have all been extremely simple and unpretentious. The question of status, scope and so forth has never, I should think, entered their minds at all. Their hidden life of love and prayer—and here surely is a capital point—has largely exceeded and entirely supported their life of active work. That, it seems to me, is the ministry which the Church so desperately wants; and if we are ever to give it, it means that our inner life towards God must be twice—no, ten, a hundred times—more vivid, constant and courageous than anything our active life may demand of us. For only thus can we ever begin to learn charity; and it is only in charity that men and women can minister to each other spiritual things. How else indeed could turbulent, half-made, self-willed creatures like ourselves hope to keep themselves at the disposal of God? If He is to find in us fresh channels of His life-giving life the proportion of our hidden prayer to our active life must be the proportion of root to tree. But are we prepared, do you think, for all that such a scheme of life will cost us; the tremendous training it will mean, and the reversal of values it involves? A return, in fact, to the values of the New Testament.

And if not, is it worth while to worry about our external scope? Movements and demands, however legitimate, can be actually dangerous if they deflect attention from the one thing that is needful to the many things that may be useful or expedient. So, if there *is* to be a new movement in the Church, a removal of barriers and a new opportunity of pastoral service for women, how terribly careful we should be that it begins in a movement of the heart; and that this movement should be, as von Hügel says, vertical first and horizontal afterwards. Don't you think that what the Church needs most, is not more and more officials but more and more people freely self-given for love? people who work from the centre, and radiate God because they possess Him; people in whom, as St. Teresa said, Martha and Mary combine. No use getting Martha that splendid up-to-date gas cooker if you have to shove Mary out of the way to find a place where it can stand.

Just notice those women in the past who have ministered with most conspicuous success to souls; the heads of our profession, the women saints. They must be our patterns, as the Curé d'Ars is the pattern for the parish priest; so we ought to keep on looking at them, looking at the top, and note what they teach. They represent, each in their own intensely distinctive way, the classic norm of women's ministry. And the first thing we observe about them is, that all are devoured by the immensity of their love and abandonment to God and Christ; and how all else flows from this, and depends on their faithful, selfless, interior adherence. And next, I think, we notice a sort of beautiful informality and freedom in their proceedings; and something which we might call a maternal and domestic quality in their method, which seems on the whole to look more towards the prophetic than the priestly way of serving God and tending souls. We see them gathering little groups about them, creating spiritual families on whom they exercise a transforming power, giving people God in a very unofficial way. Of course we know and recognize that the Church needs both these types—they complete each other—but is it not here that women seem to find their best place? As individuals surrendered to the Spirit, moving and working, under His pressure, and yet with great freedom and originality, within the institutional frame?

And next observe how quiet and hidden on the whole their best work is; and how sometimes when it develops and becomes public and they get a status—and especially when they begin to tell people in general what they ought to do and how things ought to be done, and the mother of souls becomes a reformer—they seem to charm us less, and tell us less of God. Most of us, I think, are definitely at our best in a limited environment; and it is only our best we want to give, isn't it? Our home-making talents and our instinct for nurture, teaching, loving—the power of concentrating on the individual, on the weak or the damaged, the intuitive touch on character and the understanding of it—these are the points at which women have something of real value to give to pastoral work. It is surely not when St. Hildegarde becomes a public figure, a great woman, and enters the sphere of controversy, or when Elizabeth Fry makes a semi-royal progress through Europe, stiff with black silk and consciousness of her own vocation, that we feel them most to be agents of God. Then the interior simplicity on which all hangs seems to melt away. Even the great St. Teresa said that her five happiest years were spent hidden away in the tiny convent of St. Joseph, training her little group of daughters in the interior life.

Surely we want women to retain something of that precious suppleness, simplicity and freedom which makes us tools fit for many purposes. It is so much better just to be able to say ‘ Send me ’ without having to add ‘ where I shall have my position properly recognized, or opportunities to use my special gifts.’ It is God whom we want to get recognized; not us. If we look again at the women saints, we see that with them that is usually so. They often had immense difficulties, emerging as most of them did within a Church far more rigidly organized than ours. They often suffered from the jealousy, misunderstanding and suspicion of their contemporaries. But they did feed some sheep; and that is what matters after all. Look at St. Catherine in her little room at Siena, surrounded by her spiritual sons; or Madame Acarie fulfilling her vocation in and through her family life, and becoming the ‘ Conscience of Paris ’. Consider those great lives, burning with charity; let us measure our thoughts about the ministry of women by them. A clear recognition of the standard they set is going to help women Church workers through their ups and downs, far better than any external change in our position can do. This change may turn out to be useful and desirable ; but if the other side is lacking, it won't do much for the real life of the Church. All kinds of claimfulness are so foreign to the Christian genius, that every movement of this kind involves a certain spiritual risk ; whereas every movement towards humility and hiddenness actually increases our real value to God and the Church. This does not mean softness or inefficiency ; it merely means leaving ourselves out.

Surely it is a good thing that the two orders of service within the Church should be different : and there is a mass of social and spiritual work, teaching and guidance both individual and general, and detailed training in the interior life, in which it is certain that women can and should give far more service than they have yet done. The Church should welcome such ministry, and extend these opportunities. But even where the welcome is a little bit on the frosty side—for we know that the institutional mind is not always very elastic—that does not justify *our* making a fuss. In all those new developments of Christian method which must come, and ought to come, with changing times, I am sure that women should do, and will have to do, many new and responsible kinds of spiritual work in so far as they are fitted for it. But the fitness matters most ; that interior poise which enables us to take any job, from the most desperate to the most homely, and link up the outward action with the unchanging Eternity whose purpose we are here to serve. If a new era in women's life in the Church really is opening, do not let us come to it inwardly unprepared, because we are in such a hurry to begin. I suppose, in the first century, the Church's need of workers was just as great as ours; but St. Paul thought it was worth while to begin by hiding himself for three years in Arabia, in order that he might discover what the Spirit desired him to do. I have a feeling that we ought to do something like that. For improvement in our position, or the mere multiplication of women serving in the Church, will do nothing to extend the Kingdom unless those who enter on this career really are light-bringing souls, as von Hügel said; and they will only be that in proportion to their active self-abandonment, the extent in which they ignore their own preferences and so become sensitive to God.

So I think that efforts to defend and expand the ministry of women in the Church will be useless for the deeper purposes of the Spirit, unless there is a ceaseless recognition that usefulness in religion means usefulness to God; and usefulness to God depends upon ceaseless co-operation with Him. And this again requires a sensitiveness to the movement of the Spirit impossible without a steady and disciplined interior life of prayer. I do not mean to suggest by this that the Spirit only acts through saints. The marvellous thing is, that in the true ministry of Christendom God so constantly uses sinners; but I do think they have got to be very loving and grateful sinners, entirely free from any notions about the importance of their own status and their own work. If this temper of soul, this profound humility is sought by us, then I should feel the future as regards the ministry of women was absolutely safe. Without it, we should perhaps be wise to ponder the advice which the saintly Abbé Huvelin gave to a distinguished lady of our own communion who consulted him about her numerous religious activities : 'Madame, distrust your own zeal for doing good to others'.

THE SPIRITUAL SIGNIFICANCE OF THE OXFORD MOVEMENT

I

IN the course of what Dr. Sparrow Simpson has called 'its laborious and sacrificial career', the influence of the Oxford Movement has gradually spread, till there is now no corner of the Church of England which it has failed in some degree to affect. The question of its spiritual significance must therefore concern all Anglicans, perhaps even all Englishmen; and by this we mean, I suppose, the degree in which it has mediated eternal life and thereby helped or hindered the production of holiness. For that after all is the ultimate spiritual aim of religious revival.

We are hardly likely to get much that is interesting or valuable from such an inquiry as this, unless we try at least to relate it to first principles. For what we are looking at is a phase in the vast history of religion; that is, God's self-revelation to men's souls by special ways and means, and man's response. Our own prejudices and preferences must stand down before this august fact; and we must try to consider its historical aspects humbly and with purity of sight. And first we notice that spiritual realism and spiritual results alone must be the acid-test of any revival. For spiritual results are worked only by the Spirit. Where they are present the movement is of God; even though disfigured by excesses or mistakes. Is there an increase of faith, hope and charity: a glad acceptance of suffering, the Cross: a spirit of austerity and renunciation: a deepening of the life of prayer? If so, we must surely say that we are truly in the presence of one of those movements of the Spirit within history, which from time to time bring fresh vigour to some branch of the Church. For these are marks of the supernatural life.

It is plainly not enough for this purpose merely to examine and base our judgement on the devotional value of certain revived practices, or even on the heroic achievements of certain saintly souls: for such facts point beyond themselves, and cannot be understood in isolation. To see the Oxford Movement, its hundred years of life and growth, in spiritual regard, we must give full value to the undoubted fact that it began as a deliberate attempt to recover the historical and institutional elements of religion; a restoration of our broken links with tradition, a knitting up of the dropped stitches in our bit of the seamless robe. This would not have happened, had there not arisen in certain spiritually sensitive minds, a deep sense of something lacking in the English Church life of a century ago; something which the Evangelical revival in its zenith had brought back to many individuals, but not to the corporate life of the Church. In other words, it began with the secret action of the Holy Spirit on certain characters. At the heart of the

Movement we find not merely clever people or learned theologians but hidden saints like Keble and Hurrell Froude; men with a firm hold on religious essentials, and sufficiently selfless to remain true to the Church of their baptism in circumstances of great difficulty and pain.

The Evangelical Revival had revealed anew the depth and possibilities of personal religion. The Oxford Movement, initiated by souls in whom personal religion was a consuming passion, began at the other end; by an attempt to bring back lapsed elements in the Church of England and re-establish its corporate status as a part of the Divine Society. Thus it provided, as the Evangelical Revival had failed to do, a spiritual home within which personal religion of many sorts and kinds, from the most profound to the most naïve, could find shelter and food. The result of this is now seen, in developments of which the first Tractarians did not dream, and of which the possibilities are not exhausted yet. These developments followed gradually on the re-discovery of corporate and Catholic Christianity in its richness and power—the Church, as the traditional unit and essential institution. This conception is now in some degree familiar to all of us, whether we value it or not; so that we find it difficult to realize what the religious landscape was, on which Keble looked out when he preached his epoch-making sermon a hundred years ago.

An understanding of the significance of the Oxford Movement therefore presupposes an understanding of what the true object of a religious institution is.

In the largest and deepest sense, I suppose, it exists to maintain and carry forward within history all those spiritual truths and spiritual practices which make men sensitive to God: to manifest Eternity, teach worship, and so to open and keep open paths between the unseen and the seen. The religious institution, the visible Divine Society, gathering up and preserving all the spiritual wisdom and spiritual culture of the past, provides food, warmth and shelter, a home atmosphere, a corporate religious life, a share in the common treasures, for each new Christian soul. A century ago this great vision—and with it any realistic sense of continuity with the Universal Church—had almost faded out of Anglican Christianity; and the first phase of the Oxford Movement was mainly concerned with its restoration. From that restoration all the other spiritual results have flowed. For a realistic belief in the Living Church was soon found to involve a new emphasis on the sacred reality and importance of that sacramental life which had been from the first central to Catholic Christianity. Through this the secret vivid sense of devotedness to the Person of Christ, which is the true growing point of personal religion and had been the strength of the Evangelical Movement, was enriched by a further deep and realistic sense of sharing the total life, visible and invisible, of a Body maintained by one Spirit, serving one Master, and fed from one Source. For the Catholic conception of churchmanship really consists in taking the 12th chapter of *Romans* quite literally.

And next, this re-discovery of the whole Christian tradition and practice in its integrity, brought with it a new appreciation of the disciplined life, as the necessary foundation of any full and deep spiritual life. And as a result of this renewed understanding of interior ways, this deliberate austerity of life and generous spirit of self-dedication, there appeared once more as the product and the glory of the Church in England heroic lives, both corporate and individual, of the genuine saintly type: a revival of the Religious Life of poverty, chastity and obedience, and great souls to remind the rank and file of what human nature can do and be, when it is utterly self-given to the purposes of God.

So here we have four major results of the Oxford Movement to which the word 'spiritual' can reasonably be applied. (1) The restoration of Catholic Tradition, the sense of the Church; (2) the revival of sacramental and liturgical worship; (3) the disciplined life; (4) sanctity. I do not suggest that any of these great realities had ever died out of English religion. They had not. But they had certainly become, as regards the Church at large, very dim in the period before *Tracts for the Times*; and were only held and practised by rare and special souls.

II

We come to the first spiritual gift which the Tractarians made to the Church; the recovery of tradition, of the sense of the Church as an objective whole, and the baptized Christian as part of a great and living body—the Body of Christ—with an organic life that stretches back into history and out into Eternity, including us in one living communion with our brothers and sisters the Saints. This conception, once it is truly grasped, removes the emphasis of religion from the devotional experience of the individual to that of the Church. And by one of those paradoxes which abound in the Christian life, this transfer of emphasis greatly deepens and enriches the experience of the individual soul; which loses its individual life to find another richer life. The Evangelical mind tends to present spiritual experience as a duet. For the Catholic mind it is, or should be, a symphony; and now English Christians heard once more the mighty orchestration of the Saints. The bringing back of this concept of the social nature of Christian spirituality into the field of practical religion has profound effects upon the soul. It is, for one thing, completely incompatible with an attenuated, comfortable, this-world Christianity. The standard of the Saints, in love, in suffering and in service, becomes the standard of the Church.

> Brothers, we are treading
> Where the Saints have trod. . . .
>
> . . . . .
>
> All one Body we, . . .
>
> O blest Communion, fellowship Divine,
> We feebly struggle—they in glory shine!

Through these and other hymns—all written by the Tractarians and their descendants, and used more and more by Christians of all types—this great organic conception of our status, condemning all pious pettiness and redeeming us from religious loneliness, has percolated to every branch of the Church; compelling a realization that the spiritual life, like any other kind of life, needs a social environment, food and atmosphere, and cannot with any hope of good health be pursued in isolation. The common idea of the mystic as a sort of holy cat-that-walks-by-himself and has no need of the common religious life, is, of course, fundamentally false. The deepest and noblest of the mystics—Rolle and Hilton, Francis, Catherine, Teresa—have found the riches of Eternity in means of grace accessible to every soul. Their significance is social. They have lived in close touch with their fellow Christians, have widely influenced others, and received influence in their turn. For invisible religion, with its intense concentration on God, soon overstrains the poor human creature, unless it is balanced and supported by a humble acceptance of visible religion, and corporate religious life. Nor indeed is such invisible religion an ideal for Christians, unless they practise it as members of the Mystical Body of Christ; that is, channels through which the Divine Charity flows out to the Church and other souls. This great lesson is very far from being fully learnt by Anglicans. But they have to thank the Tractarians for the fact that it has got back into the syllabus.

Again, the recovery of the sense of the Church has meant an ever-growing interest in our spiritual inheritance; a re-discovery of the treasures of the past. If the splendours of heroic sanctity are once more venerated, and even a little more understood, and the spiritual wisdom of the Saints, their mighty witness to the beauty and reality of God, is known and loved again, we have to thank the Oxford Movement for preparing the ground. For a recognition of all that it means to be members of a Catholic Church has meant fresh reverence for the supernatural lives that have been led within it, and a new and more intelligent recognition of the immense spiritual wealth of that tradition which is the inheritance of every Christian soul. If we compare the tone and contents of such a book as Vaughan's *Hours with the Mystics,* with its contemptuous references to 'dry old fathers', with the respectful treatment which the Saints now receive even at the hands of those who do not believe in them, we perceive one direction in which the Tractarian spirit set going a much needed reform. Did we strip the devotional bookshelf of all the works which this Movement has, directly or indirectly, produced or given back to us, and current religious literature of their all-pervading influence, we should be poor indeed.

III

Next, it is notorious that the second phase of the Movement—the form in which it rallied from the crisis of 1845 and the following years, when it was struggling for survival under the heavy blows dealt by the persecutions of its critics and the apostasy of its friends—the ground on which its chief battles were fought—was the development of sacramental and ceremonial worship; all that was rather clumsily known as 'ritualism'. Here it took more and more a direction which the Tractarians themselves had never contemplated; and perhaps would not have approved. Indeed, some of the more conservative men of the second generation did disapprove of many of the later developments. Yet this was without doubt the direction in which the new life now tended to expand. From the point of view of the interests of the spiritual life, what are we to think about that ?

First, it is clear that any developed corporate religion, of the Church type, must find some outward expression by means of ritual and ceremony, in order that it may satisfy a deep instinct of man ; and that the more solemn and objective the character of this outward expression, the more it conveys the 'beauty of the mysterious', the more it will awaken and support his religious sense. Ritual as an aim in itself must always be absurd ; and we cannot say that the Movement was or is without examples of this extravagance. But ritual as the outward sign of inward action is, in one form or another, natural and necessary to human creatures. It releases religious energy ; and both expresses and stimulates transcendental and corporate feeling. Even the Freemasons witness to the value of a common ceremonial in binding men together in loyalty to a common ideal ; and when we come to the things of the Spirit, this corporate use of a solemn ritual, taking up into one great tide of worship the devotion of the individual believers, balances the obvious danger of formalism by two immense advantages.

(1) Its emphasis is social and objective. It represents the ordered and all-inclusive action of the whole Church, visible and invisible ; adoring God and supplicating God, for Himself alone. It is, as St. Benedict called it, the *Opus Dei* ; done, not because it does us good, not because we want something, but for Him.

It is done because it is meet right and our bounden duty to make, as a group, this small response to the Divine Charity. Here men and women of all types and levels of enlightenment find common ground and a common task, with Angels and Archangels and all the company of Heaven praising and magnifying one Holy Name. Thus liturgic worship is the great school of theocentric religion; and should be a complete cure for self-interested piety and devotional pettiness.

(2) Next to this in importance is the fact that ceremonial worship gives religious value and religious opportunity to the whole of man's mixed nature, body, mind and spirit. It meets him where he is, and takes him as he is—a finite being with a certain capacity for the infinite—a creature of sense and of soul. It uses rhythm and gesture, contact, sight and speech, not only the bit of us which we like to call spiritual, in the approach to God. Whilst we are in this life, we can never of course get rid of the close partnership of body and spirit; and in the Incarnation Christians find this partnership blessed and endorsed by God. In our strange, rich, human experience nature and supernature are distinct, but not divided. God the invisible and ineffable shows Himself and speaks to us in natural ways, and by the consecrated use of homely things. Thus we set up a very dangerous dualism if we try to put sense and spirit in opposite camps; and this fact must control our religious practice. As spirit must enter into the life of the body if we are to be fully human; so too the body must play its part in the spirit's life. This principle, now made familiar to us by von Hügel and other

religious philosophers, may not in that form have been clear to the Anglican revivers of ritual. But it explains the fruitfulness of their work; and the fact that in spite of much that was extreme and provocative, its influence in a modified form has penetrated all branches of the Church, so that few would now feel at home at an average service of the pre-Tractarian type.

More and more we are realizing that Christianity in its richness, its complete penetration of life, cannot find adequate expression on invisible levels alone. And being what we are, it is just this appeal to the whole of us, this sacramental mingling of sense and spirit—turning the whole man Godward, and emphasizing the deep mystery of our life—which as a matter of fact gives the spirit its best chance, and provides that environment in which the life of prayer can flourish best. Believers in an Incarnational religion ought not to find this strange: but a hundred years ago it was an idea which had become entirely foreign to English Christianity. We begin then to see the significance of that intense ceremonial phase through which the Oxford Movement passed, and which still appears to many people its outstanding and to some its most objectionable characteristic. Though it was a phase the pioneers had not conceived of, and with which their sympathy would not have been great, without it the Oxford Movement would never have moved far from University precincts, lost its highbrow character, or developed all its devotional possibilities.

That concern with ritual has still a real importance in promoting the interests of holiness: the unique goal of all Christian life, whether Catholic or Evangelical. It is not, as is often supposed, an aesthetic question. It goes far deeper than that, and arises out of our belief in the nature of God and nature of Man. For ritual, where genuine, is always a dramatic expression of doctrine. It is one of the Church's great weapons in her ceaseless war against a merely utilitarian and ethical religion, and has proved to be a main channel through which the sense of the supernatural has re-entered Anglican life. It was not easy for the average Christian to experience the 'sense of the numinous' in the average Church service of 100 years ago. We easily forget what battles were fought and what sufferings undergone by those who insisted on a standard of public worship and of reverence now taken for granted everywhere. The mere opening of a church for service on a weekday—even a major saint's day—preaching in a surplice, reciting the prayer for the Church Militant, using flowers, or such ordinary pieces of church furniture as the credence table or the lectern; these were all occasions for persecution in the stormy forties and later still.

As to reverence for the Sacraments, one incident is enough to show the depth to which this had fallen in the early years of the century. Charles Simeon, as a Cambridge undergraduate, attended the Easter Eucharist in King's College Chapel. At the end of the service the celebrant gave to him and his fellow students some of the Consecrated Elements which remained over. Simeon knelt to receive them, and covered his face with his hands. He looked up, to find the clergyman laughing at this strange display of enthusiasm. If such an incident as this has now become impossible in any part of the Anglican Church, the credit for the change must go to the Oxford Movement, which—largely by its emphasis on ceremonial order—has made religious realism and the reverence that goes with it the standard of behaviour, and not the special possession of fervent souls. For among modern religious development directly due to the Tractarians, we must include the realistic acceptance of the plainly-declared truths of the Prayer Book, especially the entirely uncompromising language of the *Sanctus* and the Prayer of Oblation ; and the tendency to restore such ancient liturgic features as the *Kyrie Eleison* and the *Agnus*—not out of a mere love of medievalism, but because of their spiritual significance, their place in the total movement of worship. And that which men receive through their religious practices, is conditioned by the reverence and awe which they bring to them.

This does not mean that in the central place which they gave to Eucharistic devotion the Tractarians were inventing or importing some new thing. Here they had with them many of the saints of the Evangelical revival. John Wesley's sacramental fervour is well known, and frequent communion was a rule with the first Methodists. The same devotional temper is found in more surprising places. ' In the forenoon ', says the great Presbyterian, David Brainerd, in one place, ' while I was looking on the sacramental elements . . . my soul was filled with light and love, so that I was almost in an ecstasy.' Charles Simeon and Henry Martyn—so accessible to what he called the ' mysterious glories of religion '—can be quoted in the same sense. But these individual enlightenments were without effect on the common Church life. By the Oxford Movement this devotion, at once so transcendental and so intimate, which—central to primitive Christianity—never dies out in the Church, was brought out, developed, articulated anew to history and to doctrine; and once more made accessible to the blessed company of faithful people. The fervour, the deepened experience of prayer, the disciplined life and heroic charity which were among the most obvious spiritual fruits of the Movement; all these are closely related to the fact that frequent access to the sacraments became more and more a part of the normal routine of Anglican Church life, heightening religious sensitiveness and feeding both the corporate and the sacrificial aspect of Christian experience.

This emphasis on Eucharistic devotion was and is fiercely attacked as a mere imitation of Rome. But it was as a matter of fact a return to New Testament standards and practice; which, so far as the rank and file of the faithful were concerned, had died out for many centuries in both the Eastern and Western Church. The Tractarians were the pioneers of frequent Communion for the laity in modern Christendom; and it is interesting to note that the Roman Catholic Church is now treading the path which they, at the cost of much misunderstanding and in the teeth of actual persecution, were really the first to clear. It is on record that in St. Paul's Cathedral on Easter Day, 1800, there were six communicants. Compare this with the life of the twentieth-century cathedral;

with its daily celebrations, its rich sense of history, articulated to all the interests, activities and needs of the modern world. All this has grown and is growing very slowly ; but it springs from that seed which was planted, at the cost of great suffering, 100 years ago.

Whenever we find churches kept open for prayer and meditation, reminding us that the House of God is also the home of Man, and we discover on entering that welcoming atmosphere peculiar to a place of prayer—whenever the service is of such a character that it overcomes our sluggishness and incapacity and lifts us towards God—we might remember that it is to the Oxford Movement and those who suffered for it that we owe these and many other things.

We may allow then that the Oxford Movement has meant for English religion the restoration of two great essentials of spiritual life. It has given a renewed contact with history and tradition, bringing new access to the vast common treasury of the Church, and a new appreciation of all we have to learn from those who have gone before. It has revived that rich liturgic and sacramental worship in which, as in some living work of art, the Church's corporate life of adoration and sacrifice is expressed. All this has meant—or rather is meaning, for there is much work to be done yet—a gradual penetration of the Anglican mind by the profound truth that God works through history, and that a great religious tradition, gathering the insights and experiences of countless souls, is one of the chief instruments through which He feeds and moulds the spirit of man.

IV

But the final test of a religious movement is not to be sought in the realms of doctrine and practice, but in the souls that it forms. The promotion of holiness—this alone can guarantee any institution's spiritual worth. For Christianity is life ; 'eternal life lived in the midst of time '. And the question is, do we find this life being produced among us more richly and more generally, and are the Alpine heights of prayer and self-sacrifice more frequently attained, as the result of those changes which the Oxford Movement set going in the English Church ? It is difficult to approach this question without bias : but I think we must answer it in the affirmative. Certainly the Christian spiritual life in its full beauty has never died out. No branch of the Church has ever been without its hidden saints. The Evangelical revival produced great souls of the temper of Charles Simeon and Henry Martyn, heroic missionaries, devoted servants of the poor. Yet we are aware as we read their lives of how many of these struggled for existence in isolation ; quite ignorant of those spiritual ancestors with whom they had so much in common, or the meaning of the experiences through which they passed, and obtaining from the Church of their day the minimum of shelter, support and food. Baron von Hügel has said, in a well-known passage, that 'Souls who live an heroic spiritual life within great religious traditions and institutions, attain to a rare volume and vividness of religious insight, conviction and reality '—far more seldom achieved by the religious individualist.

The history of the English Church during the last century, especially the section most influenced by the Oxford Movement, illustrates this saying in a striking way. Newman, says Dean Church, arrived at the conviction that Devotion and Sacrifice—the substance of Holiness—are the authentic marks of a living Church. He sought these graces for himself where he saw them already existent. The friends whom he left behind strove at great cost to express them in action where they were. Thus they not only set going the renovation of the Church of England, but also lit before its altar the lamp of sanctity. In the greatest of the many dedicated lives that Church has since produced, we seem to recognize once more the authentic note of a sanctity that emerges within a society, a Church, conforms to the family pattern, is supported and fed by the supernatural life indwelling that Church; and so reaches a solid maturity of holiness which is beyond the span of religious individualism, however intense. We surely feel this quality, for instance, in Father Richard Benson, the founder of Cowley; or in Father Wainright of Dockland, whose fifty years' devoted service of the poor was the result of an early reading of the lives of St. Vincent de Paul and the Curé d'Ars, and was nourished by that long period of rapt devotion before the altar with which each working day began. In some, too, of those heroic women who brought back the life of the religious orders to the English Church.

This gradual revival of the religious orders, and the re-establishment among us of the steadfast routine of the monastic life, subordinating all things to the *Opus*

Dei, the corporate worship of God—this is a spiritual phenomenon to which we hardly attach all the importance it deserves. It has come bit by bit, as the necessary expression of one strand in that new and rich life which sprang from the Oxford Movement; bringing with it the spirit of wholesale dedication, whether to the enclosed life of heroic prayer, or the mixed life of action inspired by contemplation. As the great orders of the past sprang into being through the personal initiative and unlimited faith of a few determined souls, so the history of their modern counterparts is full of the romance of the consecrated life. The great Community of St. Mary the Virgin at Wantage, with branches in every part of the world, began with a couple of friends in a country cottage struggling to live the Religious Life. Three heroic women establishing themselves in a dilapidated loft 'in literal acceptance of the Gospel precepts' to nurse the sick poor in their homes, founded in the teeth of insult and persecution the Sisterhood of St. Margaret at East Grinstead. It is surely a great matter that this life of absolute consecration, this literal obedience to the demand to 'Leave all', should thus have returned to the Church of England; to reprove and to stiffen our easy-going religiosity, by its vivid witness to the unlimited claim of God on the souls that He calls, the power and attraction of the other-worldly life, the ghostly energy which is released by entire renunciation, for the support of souls and the battle against sin. It has meant for all brought into contact with it a new recognition of what it can mean to be in body, soul and spirit a servant of the Crucified, a reasonable and living sacrifice ; and has already shown us what human nature can become, when it leaves all and gives itself without limit to the purposes of God, whether in the life of service or the life of prayer. The presence within the Church of these dedicated lives, and the production of that holiness, that poetry of goodness which is the fruit of dedication —this is surely a marvellous witness to the reality and attraction of God.

It is often assumed that God can bring forth His saints anywhere, and give them their meat in due season ; in other words that the emergence and development of spiritual genius has very little to do with institutional religion. But history and psychology seem to oppose this view. The great saints have mostly arisen within the religious system they were destined to purify or adorn, and their debts to the deepest and most stable elements in that system —especially its tradition of prayer and self-discipline —have been great. Saints, if they are to develop their fullest capacity, need much education. The appearance among us of heroic souls, the many decisive vocations to poverty, chastity and obedience—and also the widespread desire for a revival of the life of prayer, and uneasy realization of its necessity, which has now covered England with a network of Retreat Houses and brings eager pupils to all who offer instruction on the inner life—all this I am sure is very closely connected with the restoration of the forgotten ideal of Christian asceticism in its true sense, which we owe ultimately to the Tractarians. For this restoration of the tradition of Christian austerity, the severe standards of life and unmitigated moral claim of the full Catholic outlook—this renewed appreciation of the costly character of all deep religion—has alone made possible the development of those men and women of prayer who are themselves actual channels of the Spirit and means of grace. It is not for nothing that his fellow-workers in East London were accustomed to call Father Wainright the Eighth Sacrament: for wherever he went, that small untiring figure seemed to bring the power of God. The interior life as a practical fact, and the discipline of thought and action which goes with it—all this re-entered English Church life with the Tractarians. It had, and is having, its effect, in the formation of souls which without this spiritual culture would hardly have developed their full capacity whether for contemplation or for service. The modern world, knowing the worth and necessity of specialists in science and the arts, should value these spiritual specialists more than it is at present inclined to do. They are the eyes and ears of the Body of Christ.

Baron von Hügel was fond of saying, that in the true order of religious development the Church comes first and the mystics afterwards. When Peter and John—types of the institutional and the mystical elements of Christianity—ran together to the Holy Sepulchre, John the seer reached the mystery first; but it was Peter, the Church, who went in first. So the intuition of the spiritual realist may arrive first; but his fullest lights and convictions come to him when he follows where the Church has first trod. Then he exercises his true function within the Mystical

Body: which is not to have strange and individual adventures, to dart off as it were into the Eternal, but rather to enter into and explore ever more fully the wonder and significance of the revealed. Something of this sort seems to me to have happened—or rather to be still happening—in connexion with that great English revival of Church-religion which began 100 years ago. And I do not think either its friends or its critics will come to an understanding of its true quality and meaning, until they have considered it from this point of view. Great movements within history unfold their deep implications stage by stage. Although appearances may sometimes deceive us, there is as a matter of fact nothing hurried and cataclysmic about them. They partake of the great divine rhythm which we discover within all life. First the blade, then the ear, then the full corn in the ear. This was true of the Primitive Church; so closely dependent on the Spirit's guidance yet exhibiting almost at the beginning characters which we should scarcely regard as the peculiar marks of a spiritual Church. For it is apparent that the first great impulse—often claimed as wholly non-dogmatic and non-ecclesiastical—led, as a matter of fact, to the prompt formation of a theology and an institution, and very soon to the development of a certain ritual practice. It was within the home thus provided, and in dependence upon that rich tradition which it handed on, that the spiritual life took root and flowered in the various love and holiness of the Saints.

So too in each succeeding period. The Middle Ages consolidate, even over-consolidate the institution, and give through St. Thomas an absolute precision to the theology: and from within a Church thus intensely organized, utterly Petrine, again the mystical life in its freedom and beauty, the pure heroic passion for Christ and God, the energy of sacrifice, break out with power. The great family of the fourteenth-century mystics are truly the children, even though sometimes the unruly children, of the medieval Church. Careful study will convince most students of this; and show that even the repressive elements of that Church acted as a useful check on individual intuition. Again, the Reformation—even though we are now learning to appreciate the genuinely religious character of Luther's genius—was first of all concerned with the overhaul of theology and institutional practice. And perhaps because in all this there was so much that was crude and controversial, because the Church-type with its warm inclusiveness was departed from and the sect-type with its dangerous individualism took its place—above all because the ideals of asceticism were ruthlessly flung away—we miss here the depth and reality, the self-abandoned beauty, of the spiritual life as seen in the Saints. Only in the seventeenth century does it begin to reappear, struggling for existence in religious surroundings which are rather suggestive of the old family mansion that has been broken up into a series of not very convenient flats. In the Latin countries the Counter-Reformation followed much the same path. St. Peter put his house in order; and the spirit of St. John emerged again. First the Council of Trent and the Jesuits; then the revival of the religious orders and marvellous outburst of spiritual life—the missionary saints and the mystical saints—Françis Xavier and Marie Martin, Teresa and John of the Cross, Francis de Sales and Madame Acarie. Certainly diagrams of this kind must not be pressed too far. The free action of God on souls is manifest at every point in history, and takes little account of our neat ideas. But on the whole and in a general sense we find that the genuine revival of corporate and traditional Christianity in its fullness provides the environment within which the spiritual life develops best.

In the remarkable growth of Church religion which sprang from the Oxford Movement, and has produced and is still producing developments and results of which the Tractarians themselves never dreamed, we seem to detect the same order of growth. First the intense concentration on history and tradition: the recovery of the Catholic idea, and of neglected parts of our great inheritance. Then the institutional development; the concentration on ritual and ceremony, sometimes carried to absurd lengths, yet giving once again a stimulus and a vehicle for devotion and so enriching both the corporate and the personal life towards God. Then the intellectual reconstruction which began with *Lux Mundi*; and now has to its credit the work of a brilliant group of theological scholars. And, emerging among all this very quietly, yet steadily gathering way, the supernatural life of prayer, sacrifice, love; feeding on these other various factors, incarnating itself in many different types, both active and contemplative, and many different careers. And let the philanthropic Christian, always a little bit tempted to put the Second Commandment before the First, take note of the fact that only the philanthropic work which is done directly or overtly for God, and draws its energy from the communion of the Spirit, glows with the selfless passion that gives power. A theocentric religion is the best starting-point for that fundamental reconstruction of society which all now have at heart: and a sacramental religion gives both philosophic sanction and spiritual support to its ideals. The rich amalgam of history and spirituality —the love of man which is born of the Love of God, and therefore shares in the energy of the Divine Charity—this is the Christian hope of the future, and perhaps it is the world's hope too. The neglected elements which the Oxford Movement brought back into English Christianity, are surely those best calculated to feed and steady that flame.

ST. FRANCIS AND FRANCISCAN SPIRITUALITY[1]

IT is a desperate task, at this time of day, to attempt to say anything about St. Francis of Assisi which is not familiar and even over-familiar to all of us. And yet, as the natural world holds to the very end something in reserve for us, and can show us new beauty and new meaning, again and again, with a freshness, a shock of delight, that keeps pace with our real growth ; so it is, I think, with the contemplation of great souls. Here too, because their secret life must always immeasurably exceed our own, there are always fresh paths of approach awaiting us, and always fresh discoveries to be made. That which we know of them in general, is merely the sum total of that which their various lovers have so far seen in them : and that is always a limited vision, conditioned by the seeing mind, of a mystery which stretches away beyond our focus, to be lost to view in the great mystery of life. In this partial way we know something of the effect of great souls upon

[1] Walter Seton Memorial Lecture, delivered at University College, London, 17 January 1933.

history, their relation to their environment, their special teaching, influence, and charm: and from these various pictures our minds construct a sort of composite photograph, which we only too easily mistake for the real man.

Thus St. Francis has again and again been shown to us, as—among many other things—the humble penitent, the bridegroom of Lady Poverty, the troubadour of God, the enemy of capitalism, the ecstatic of La Verna, the successful revivalist, the brother of the birds, and the poet of the Canticle of the Sun. And yet a rather blurred, even if attractive picture, seems to result from the attempt to combine all these in one figure, perhaps because we still lack the dominant image which shall harmonize them; the picture of the spiritual Francis, the intensely living creature possessed and devoured by a secret love, who finds a fragmentary yet real expression in all these symbolic attitudes and deeds.

For we know that in dealing with St. Francis we are dealing, not with a small neat mind of a particular sort, capable of analysis, but with a great soul who was a genuine source of more abundant life to all who came within his sphere of influence. St. Francis, however else we regard him, is shown by history to have been one of those creative personalities which break out from time to time with disconcerting suddenness within the human scene; to reveal new spiritual possibilities within life, and initiate a new spiritual growth, which flowers in a wide variety of souls. These creative personalities, in their abrupt appearance, their entirely unconscious originality and freedom, defy all our attempts to classify or to define them. For they are real, individual, intensely living men and women; who are made ardent by a supernatural glow, and become channels of a supernatural energy. They stand in the gap between the hidden Perfect and the imperfect world, and love not one but both; revealing within history the absolute goodness, applying the absolute standard, and communicating the absolute life, because they are saturated by it, because they cannot conceive existence except in relation to it, not because they have new and interesting opinions about it. This is why we really cannot hope to make much sense of their activities, or relate their outward to their inward life, unless we accept, at least as an hypothesis, the passion and the conviction by which they always live; the passion for God, and the conviction of the absolute priority of the Eternal, the vivid presence and ceaseless pressure of God within the world. Take away this, which is the whole meaning of his life, and the saint looks insignificant, and often rather silly too. He is like one of those hats which are everything on the head, nothing in the hand. Father Wilfred Knox observes in his life of St. Paul, that from the point of view of contemporary Pagan culture, Paul would have appeared as a small and unimpressive Jew, creeping from ghetto to ghetto; yet he bore in his bosom the seed of the Catholic Church. So too St. Francis, if he reappeared amongst us, would certainly seem small and of no reputation—even perhaps intolerably tiresome—to those who could not recognize the supernatural flame of holiness within the homely lantern of his love.

So it may be, that what is chiefly lacking in our composite portrait of St. Francis, with its invincible attraction, its disconcerting contrasts, and its refusal to fit into our gallery of types, is the subjection of all the elements of the picture to this one overruling fact of Holiness, which gave his life its supernatural intention and supernatural worth. And it may be worth while to look at him again, with this as our controlling thought. The most enthusiastic modern admirers of Francis generally seem to fall into two classes, and arrive at their view-point from two opposite directions; and were we not so dim and vague about fundamentals, so terribly willing to be satisfied with the easy and picturesque, we should perceive the completeness of the contrast between them. For one —the naturalistic school—finds all that really matters about him on the outside; in the give-and-take between Francis and his environment. The other—the supernatural school—finds all that really matters in the inside; in the give-and-take between Francis and the unseen realities of his faith. The naturalistic admirers often seem to think that he is all the more a saint, because he differs from their notion of the normal kind of saint; and they stress these differences all the time. But there is not, of course, any such thing as a normal kind of saint. A saint is just a human being released from the love of self, and enslaved by the love of God. Any kind of human being will do for that, and the less conventional he is the better for the purpose of his new career; for the spirit makes strange demands upon its instruments. The supernatural school, on the contrary, seeks and finds in Francis, in a high degree, what it regards as the essential marks of sanctity: a single-minded devotion to the purposes of God, a transforming influence on souls, a total oblation of personality. Absorbed in these great matters, it does not take particular notice of the things that give special delight to the Franciscan naturalist. But the supernaturalist too forgets something; and surely a very important something. He tends to ignore all those human aptitudes and tendencies, those fresh and unconventional judgements of and responses to the world of things, with its good and evil, joy and pain, which form the raw material of holiness: aptitudes and tendencies which become, when transmuted by the fire of love, part—and a very lovely part—of the saint's living sacrifice to the purposes of the Infinite Life.

It is true in a sense to say that a Christian saint is a new creature. But he is a new creature for which all the old material has been used; and the character of this material will condition his type. For a saint is not an angel, but a solid human being of body, soul and spirit, physically and psychologically conditioned, and operating in space and time. And perhaps it will give us a fresh view at least of one aspect of St. Francis, if we ask what the raw material of personality was in his case. In other words, what sort of person would Francis have been, if he had grown up unconverted; had not been driven to capitulate to the unseen love? Where should we have looked in the world of his day, for the sort of man who is foreshadowed by his early, unconverted life? There is surely not much doubt about that. Francesco

Bernadone was, from the world's point of view, a most disconcerting and attractive creature. He had a very high index of aesthetic sensibility, a hunger for romance. He responded with joy to every wayside beauty, and shrank with a peculiar horror from hideous and repulsive things ; a sensibility which was afterwards transmuted into an infinite compassion and sympathy for all life. The life of the senses—colour, music, taste, fragrance, texture—meant much to Francis. The living sacrifice he offered was rich with possibility of delight ; for he was capable of seeing and feeling far more than most men in that created world which is all that most men feel and see, and brought a child's spontaneity and eagerness, a child's completeness of response to every experience, simple or sublime, which it offered him.

Add to this the important fact that his response to these experiences always tended to have a dramatic character. He had an immense need of movement and expression. The temper of soul which gave us the Christmas crib at Greccio appears again and again in all the chief incidents of his career. With him, every interior movement and interior light tends to have its outward expression. We find examples of this on every page of the Franciscan story. Such symbolic gestures as the stripping off of his clothes in the streets of Assisi, or the literal mending of the ruined church, the kissing of the leper, the preaching to the birds, or the exquisite scene at the close of his life, when he fed his brethren with blessed bread : these things are simply expressions of St. Francis's general attitude to existence. He is equally at home in the visible and the invisible world, and lives in both at once. Both are full of friendly presences, from Brother Sun to Sister Death. His very practice of poverty has its dramatic, indeed its sacramental aspect. His life might be regarded as a continuous mystery play; and has proved richer in pictorial incidents than the legend of any other saint.

If beyond this we consider that total indifference to class and convention which makes short work of respectability, takes off its clothes without concern in the open street, and sees no difficulty about adopting the free life of a tramp, remove from all this the religious colour, and look at it with innocence of eye, it is easily recognized as part of the characteristic make-up of the artist-type; perhaps specially of the dramatic poet. The unconverted Francis, delightful if somewhat bewildering in his versatility and quickly changing moods, is still a familiar figure in what used to be called Bohemian society. His parents are often solid business people, who cannot understand his irresponsibility and violent reaction from the family ideals. Surely too we get something of the social flexibility of the artist, his easy friendliness with all classes and all types, in Celano's casual saying of Francis: 'More sanctified than the saints, amongst sinners he was as one of themselves.' And when we add to all this the incurable troubadour temper, the intense love of rhythm and music, which made him regard the First Companions as above all else the Lord's minstrels and urge on them the duty of song, and the 'French-like rejoicings' which broke out as the natural expression of his own fervour for

God, we can hardly doubt that one of the wedding gifts which Francesco Bernadone made to the Lady Poverty was a laurel crown he might have worn.

Nor is Francis the only natural artist in the Celestial Rose. Here, among others, he has as his companion one of the greatest—yet apparently one of the least Franciscan—of all Christian mystics, that mighty transcendentalist St. John of the Cross: a fact which it is worth while to recollect. The poet of the 'Canticle of the Sun', and the poet of 'The Dark Night of the Soul' are alike in this, that their intense artistic sensibility gave its special quality of realism to their contemplation of supernatural things. As the great artist shows us in this world a beauty we cannot see or hear without his help; so, by the transfiguration of that same quality, these in their different ways show us a spiritual richness, truth, and beauty which we cannot perceive alone.

Of this sort, then, I think, was the natural Francis before the Divine Charity seized and transformed him; and perhaps the curious fact that this most impassioned and realistic of Christians has become specially the saint of the unchurched, and is loved by thousands who would hardly accept one of his governing beliefs, is closely connected with his natural make up. For he is somehow felt, as other saints are not, to reveal a beauty and significance in the visible world, a perfection of adjustment to its life, that we had lost or failed to realize before. He brings to men and women that harmony with life for which they crave; and does this in a way that is peculiarly winning, at once poetic and homely, because he is, at one and the same time, a poet, an artist, and a saint. Out of our confusions, difficulties, and anxieties, and the unreal sufferings we manufacture for ourselves, he awakes us to the inexhaustible charm, the authentic beauty of a human life so loving and so single-minded, so humble and so courageous, that it cut clean through the web of convention, and came out into the free air of reality. A life, it is true, which contained much suffering and almost continual hardship; but found in these the material of Perfect Joy. Certainly the wide popularity of Francis owes something to the persuasive charm of certain incidents in that life; as the wide popularity of any beautiful soul always owes something to the gracious actions in which that beauty is expressed. This must be so in our mixed world of sense and spirit, where the appeal of the soul is made through the veil of the flesh. But that is not enough. We must go deeper if we want to find the source of that creative power which history proves that Francis possessed; that transforming influence which he exercised and continued to exercise after his bodily death on a multitude of souls of different types. And here we must make the transition from the natural to the spiritual Francis, and try to see together the artist and the mystical saint.

All readers of the letters of Baron von Hügel will remember the penetrating and unconventional sayings of his director, the saintly Abbé Huvelin: and among them one which strikes us on first reading as a paradox. Huvelin said to the Baron on one occasion in answer to a question which is not reported to us, 'Yes, there have been saints, and even great saints, of your type. St. Francis of Assisi—I don't mean the Franciscans!—*there* is a saint wholly cast in the mould of life and movement, light and warmth!' Those who knew the great scholar-saint, or know him from his profound and often difficult teaching, and those who think they know the spirit of St. Francis, will feel baffled by this judgement. For where are we to find the likeness between the vast and deep intellect, the awe-struck spirit of von Hügel, and the little shabby penitent with his inexhaustible vitality, his bursts of poetry, his child-like friendliness to every living creature, his transfiguration of squalor, his utter contempt for mere scholarship, his equal acceptance of joy and of suffering, his unlimited and incandescent love? Nevertheless this is a judgement from within. It is the opinion of a saint—a realist, for whom God was everything—about two other saints, also realists for whom God was everything; and neither of whom were able to exclude any aspect of His creation from the sphere of their interest and their love. Plainly it is not an opinion based on surface characters, but on some interior likeness which entirely escapes the casual glance. What was it?

I think perhaps it was this. Both the medieval friar and the modern scholar were penetrated by a sense of the realness, more the sacredness, of the natural as well as the supernatural order; as something which was not to be fled from, but to be loved without possessiveness, with an unlimited and humble tenderness cleansed of all desire. This is not the outlook of the pious naturalist or the higher pantheist. It is the outlook of the genuine Christian supernaturalist, who replaces nature where it belongs—in the Heart of God—and is conscious of His supporting presence through and in the web of life. ' God,' said von Hügel, ' is a stupendously rich Reality ; He is the God of Nature, as well as the God of Supernature.' St. Francis would have understood and welcomed that. Every movement of his life declares its truth. Hence come the Franciscan attitude of reverence and delight towards the finite world in which we live ; and the humble and friendly love of all those creatures whom von Hügel, in terms St. Francis would surely have echoed, called ' our little relations, the lesser children of God '.

By a sort of poetic intuition transfigured by heavenly love, St. Francis arrived at just that balanced sense of the sacramental value of the finite and temporal, the world of our daily experience on one hand, and the over-ruling mystery and attraction of the Infinite and Eternal world of Spirit over against us on the other hand, which lies at the very heart of von Hügel's philosophy of religion. He can never be explained on a basis of shallow immanentism, nature mysticism, or any other reduction of religion's full demand. No one will understand Franciscan spirituality, who does not bear in mind that awe-struck sense of the Transcendent, the Eternal, which emerges now and then to warn us that we have in St. Francis something more than a pure and delightful soul who found God in nature and nature in God. It is only when we refuse the temptation to simplify, to ignore the bits we do not understand, and put side by side some of the contrasting strands in his experience, and that of his greatest followers, that we begin to realize how rich this experience was, how completely it was penetrated and controlled by the metaphysical craving for God; though we may be sure that St. Francis would never have given his ruling passion this name. I take it that one of the most deeply significant incidents for a real understanding of his mind, is that strange scene in the house of Bernardo Quintavalle; where a converted poet, still hardly more than a lad, is heard murmuring all night the single awful question, 'My God and All! what art thou, and what am I?': the problem which, once it lays hold upon the spirit, is the beginning alike of adoration and of humility. That Francis is a figure very unlike the Brother of the Birds of popular sentiment. Yet only one who has thus capitulated to Reality, and discovered his own creaturely status, can truly become a Brother to the Birds.

If we take that unique revelation of the secret life of Francis, that discovery of his own place, as seriously as we should, and remember it whilst we watch the drama of his outer life—the ceaseless self-spending, the joy and the hardship, the struggles with demons, the pleasant friendship with the falcon and the pheasant, the missionary ardour and the snatches of contemplation—I think that we shall give our portrait of him a certain unity it lacked before: and a background and atmosphere without which it can never be true to life. And if we are to understand Franciscan spirituality—so various and even contradictory in its expressions, sometimes so lofty and sometimes so child-like, but always inspired by an ardent and practical love—we should always keep this scene in mind. For when we are dealing with a saint, it is not the charming gesture, but the deep experience—not what he does for men, but what is done to him by the mysterious stirrings of the Spirit, and what his response—which matters most and helps us to understand him best.

A saint is a human creature devoured and transformed by love: a love that has dissolved and burnt out those instinctive passions—acquisitive and combative, proud and greedy—which commonly rule the lives of men. Therefore we must always consider him in relation with the two supreme objects of his love; God and the World, or that special bit of the world on which he is destined to pour out his charity. And the isolated facts about St. Francis which make up our mental image, are all found when we examine them, to be simply different expressions—conditioned by his special make up—of that love which made of him, perhaps, the most unspoilt channel of the Divine generosity known to us since New Testament times. That outpouring Charity, that *Agape*, in which the manward life of God consists, transformed him by 'the kindling of his mind', as he was told in the great experience on La Verna; so that his whole life, deeply considered, was swept up to become part of the Divine action, the self-expression of the Divine Love. The varied incidents of that external life fall into place, when we learn to see them as symptoms and sacraments of this interior state, in which he solved the problem of his relation to God, 'What art thou and what am I?' When that question is asked by a poet with his eyes fully opened on reality, he can hardly stop short of the total consecration which is holiness. Here then is the source of that intense sensitiveness to all the appeals of the life that surrounded him, whether in its loveliness and movement, or in its piteous subjection to sin, evil, and disease. Birds and animals, lepers and sinners and simple loving souls, and the men of many different types who left all to follow him, are equal candidates for his interest and love. Thus we learn to understand that wide-open sympathy, in such vivid contrast to the exclusions and repressions of the monastic type.

We feel the more justified in adopting such a view of St. Francis, when we go back to the earliest records and see what the things were which struck his contemporaries as specially significant in his life. They are, I suppose, the things which would still stand out, for those whose spirits breathe the air on which he lived. For such a vision, I think the graph which records the real life of St. Francis—seen so to speak in supernatural regard—would mark two supreme points. The first point would be that in which it seemed to him that a voice spoke from the Crucifix of S. Damiano, and demanded his total dedication to its purposes. The second point would be that in which the seraph on La Verna, with its reminiscence of Isaiah's mighty Vision of Reality baptized into Christianity, and mysteriously united with the sufferings of the Cross, completed his initiation into the deep secrets of the redemptive order. That overwhelming illumination ruled the last two years of his life. Whether it was a glimpse of eternal truths, or whether we regard it as a morbid illusion, this was the supreme thing which Francis saw, loved, and believed; and that with such intensity, that the love and belief took physical form. Here he found the clue to the meaning of his own life, as a servant and agent of the unseen. The mysterious power and worth of innocent suffering, and the enlightened spirit's call to that suffering through which alone it can exercise a saving love: this is what that penetrating yet simple poetic genius of his, lifted to the supernatural order, found at the very heart of life.

His whole career, as I see it, is poised on these two strange events. The first drew him out towards the visible world, to help, mend, and serve it. The second made him the mysterious partner of an invisible rescuing love. Wherever we get him really speaking his mind, he is never far from the Cross: the underlying tension of life. 'Yes, there it is; no need to go further', said Huvelin. 'Sanctity and suffering are the same thing. You will do no good to others save in suffering and through suffering.' We draw very near the real Francis, though not very near the popular notion of Francis, when we meditate on these words. The extreme sensibility of the transfigured poet feels the world's anguish; and is always trying to make an alliance, first in one way and then in another, with the saving and self-giving forces of the Spiritual Order. It is this temper of soul which makes the most abject humiliation the material of Perfect Joy. The entire growth of Francis was towards the point at which, as that strange phrase in his legend says, he was 'transformed by the kindling of his mind into the image of the Crucified ', embracing and harmonizing in one movement of self-abandoned love, the splendour of God and the deep suffering of man. That is Charity, the outpouring passion of generous love at its full height, depth, breadth, and width; a passion which is the earnest of eternal life, and reflects back to a metaphysical source. St. Francis, says the *Fioretti* in a famous passage, offered his followers ' the chalice of life '; and those who had courage to drink it, ' saw in profound contemplation the abyss of the infinite divine light ': a strange phrase for the sort of gift which the St. Francis of popular sentiment, the little poor man, the troubadour, the animal's friend, is supposed to have made to the world. But if we ponder it, it does lead us back to the central truth of his life: the intense spiritual realism of the poet-saint, bringing fresh life and movement, light and warmth, into all his relations with things visible, just because of the completeness of his hold on things invisible. Living with simplicity in the embrace of the immensity because of his disinterested love, he shows us that union of mystery and homeliness which is the Christian solution of the paradox of life. We think, when we look at St. Francis kneeling before the first Christmas crib at Greccio, or read Jacopone da Todi's Christmas hymns, that they are showing us the child-like simplicity of their faith. But not so. They are awe-struck before the Christian paradox revealed on every altar: the greatness and littleness of love.

Those people who desire to take a naturalistic view of Francis, and of our human situation, and explain away the strangeness and the suffering and keep the love and poetry, the gaiety and charm, may produce a picture which is very flattering to our corporate pride in human nature ; but nothing which remotely resembles the portrait of St. Francis or indeed of any other saint. For in the saint, the response—the complete capitulation—to unseen realities comes first ; and all that he shows the world of Holiness is the result of this. That is not a particularly popular doctrine now—our shallow naturalism revolts from it—but the whole trend of the life of Francis proves his implicit understanding of it ; and we shall never get that life in proportion unless we try to understand it too.

When we take away the trappings, the charm and quaintness and pretty anecdotes, and all the holy Zoo business, and get down to the deep root of the matter, what we find is surely this. The real greatness of St. Francis is the same as the greatness of the Christian religion, when fully understood. For it is one thing to be a believer in Christianity, or even a courageous practitioner of its hard demands, another thing to be sensitized to all its mysterious implications : and it is just these mysterious implications which the poetic intuition and intrepid love of Francis seized and expressed in terms of human life. He reflects the very spirit of his Master in the completeness, ease, and simplicity with which he entered into our two-fold human heritage of spirit and of sense. On the one hand life and movement, light and warmth, all the activities of a homely love ; serving the sick, living with the poor, considering the birds and the flowers, and seeking to raise the hearts of men to God. On the other hand, all the tension, suffering, interior solitude which is the price of a saving love: the Cross.

When we come to examine the experience of the immediate followers of Francis—the First Companions, and those who had learned to know him through the First Companions—we find much support for this view. It is true that here the evidence might be regarded as biased, since all the most living and attractive reminiscences come to us through works which were composed in the interest of the Spiritual party, and often for controversial use. Still, there is no reason to doubt the accuracy of the general impression which they give us. For nothing less than this impression can account for the stream of spiritual life which arose from Francis: a stream which flows still, though often its course is underground for a while. To these close friends and clients of his—some of whom struggled to imitate, while others were content only to admire him—Francis was not simply a mystic who had re-discovered the evangelical poverty, freedom, and joy. What they saw in him was something far more fundamental: a re-incarnation as it were of the whole evangelical life in its completeness, its riches and poverty, suffering and beauty, the Crib and the Cross. He was one in whom, as Jacopone da Todi said plainly, 'Christ was felt to live again' and show in its perfection the right relation of man to God.

'First', says the opening chapter of the *Fioretti*, 'we must needs consider how the glorious St. Francis in all the acts of his life was conformed to Christ the

Blessed One.' All Franciscan students know that this startling sentence represents a view of Francis which was developed within a very short time of his death; and which was worked out in minute detail, reaching before the end of the thirteenth century the point marked by Jacopone da Todi's hymns to his Patriarch, where Francis is invoked as virtually a re-incarnation of Christ, so near his Pattern that even Satan was deceived. Such a claim as that points right past all the merely picturesque accidents of his life and spirituality—the troubadour spirit, the passion for poverty, the widespread love of living things—to something tremendous, something fundamental, in the impression which that small and humble figure made upon his world. He is, I believe, the only saint of whom such a thing as this has ever been suggested or said: and it was said by orthodox Catholics of another orthodox Catholic, and no one appears to have regarded it as blasphemous or extreme. Do we begin to understand St. Francis until we have given this astonishing fact full weight? I hardly think so. Other men and groups of men have set to work to re-live that Gospel life which gave human form to the Eternal Charity. No one but St. Francis left behind him the reputation of a success so genuine, that it could be said and sung of him in all sincerity 'It seemed as if Christ had come again; that very Christ who died upon the Rood'.

Now this, the rounded whole of sanctity, this mysterious and unlimited self-giving to the eternal purpose, in which charity and suffering become one thing, is what St. Francis seems to show us with a crystalline simplicity. And this is surely the key to the creative quality of his life. Without this clue, all the dramatic actions, all the gratuitous sufferings and voluntary humiliations, the deeds that enchant us and those that make us feel uncomfortable and ashamed, fall apart. They become separate and often inconsistent episodes, lacking significance. With it, they are seen as incidents in the dramatic poem which expressed in action the secret movements of his inner life. When St. Bonaventura came to systematize Franciscan spirituality, it is significant that he found in Platonic philosophy, with its contrasting worlds of eternity and time, the system which harmonized with his Patriarch's spirit best; and that, in opposition to the doctrine of St. Thomas Aquinas, he declared will and love to be the highest powers of man's soul, and the instruments of his union with God.

On this basis, we are able to understand the true nature of that spiritual heritage which St. Francis left behind him: the widely varying types of fervour and spirituality which have been claimed as representative of Franciscan mysticism. This principle illuminates and governs Franciscan poverty, Franciscan penitence, and Franciscan joy. It harmonizes the lonely contemplative life of the hermitage, and the busy active life of the tramping revivalist; trying to persuade men to cast off their entanglements, and see in God the reality of their own lives. For the peculiar note of Franciscan spirituality is neither its simplicity and charm on the one hand, nor its total contrite self-oblation on the other hand: not, to resort again to its two most characteristic devotions, either the

Crib or the Cross, but both. It is the awe-struck sense of the Eternal which gives light and warmth to its humble, creaturely, and very loving acceptance of the human scene : a profound sense of the solemn privilege of sacrifice which deepens and steadies its exultant love. And Franciscan poverty means, I think, such a quiet rejection of all superfluities, such a horror of mere possession and mere clutch, as leaves the soul of man free to apprehend that only reality of our existence, that deep and mysterious relationship with God which underlies St. Francis's question, 'What art thou, and what am I ?'

Franciscan history is full of examples of this alert and adoring sense of reality : this hold upon the double truth of our sublime yet lowly situation. Brother Giles has it ; proclaiming the immensity of God, and all man's knowledge of Him as no more than a grain snatched by a sparrow from a mountain of corn. Jacopone da Todi has it, and gives it to us in poems which stretch from the extreme of homeliness to the stammering reports of ecstacy. So has the author of the Capuchin reform, so well named by Father Cuthbert a 'visionary realist'. But nowhere perhaps do we feel it so strongly as in the scene which closed the life of that great spiritual genius Angela of Foligno. There I think, more than anywhere else, we recognize the very essence of true Franciscan mysticism—its creaturely simplicity, and its awe-struck sense of God. When she knew that she was dying, Angela called all her spiritual children to her, and blessed them and said to them, 'Make yourselves small ! Make yourselves small !' And after that she lay very still, and they heard her murmuring, ' No creature is sufficient! No intelligence, even of angels or of archangels, is sufficient!' Those who were round her asked, ' What is it, Mother, for which the intelligence even of angels and archangels is not sufficient?' And she said, ' To understand.'

RICHARD THE HERMIT

THE improvement in our modern knowledge of the medieval mystics, and our gradual progress towards an understanding of their minds, is well shown in the sort of attention now paid to the life and work of Richard Rolle of Hampole. This important religious personality, as we now know him to have been—so characteristically English in his sturdy individualism and ethical emphasis—was not only this but also one of the first of English religious poets, the author of our earliest vernacular Psalter, and a popular (though never an official) saint whose local cultus survived well into the sixteenth century. Yet so complete was the oblivion into which he had fallen, that he was not even mentioned in Dean Inge's Bampton Lectures on Christian Mysticism, which ushered in the revived interest in this subject; nor yet in his later lectures on the English Mystics. Subsequent writers began to notice Richard's existence, modernized versions of some of his works gradually appeared; and somewhat sketchy accounts of his doctrine, based upon these, have been inserted in recent books on medieval mysticism. Our genuine knowledge of Rolle, however, is mainly due to the careful labours of two scholars. First Miss Deanesly, who edited in 1915 the Latin text of his most characteristic work, the *Incendium Amoris*.[1] Next, and especially, Miss Hope Allen, who published in 1928 the important results of twenty years' patient research—including examination of the chief existing Rolle MSS.—and followed this up in 1931 by a critical selection of his English writings[2]; and in so doing has clarified and in some sense revolutionized our view of his life and personality.

Miss Allen is almost certainly the only human being of modern times—it might be safe to say, the only one since the sixteenth century—who has examined all Rolle's authentic works. She alone is therefore really competent to arrange them in series and tell us what, at each stage of his career, he thought and taught; what elements we must take into account in our attempts at reconstructing his personality and the story of his spiritual development. Hitherto, such attempts have necessarily been made mainly on the basis of the *Incendium* and the three English treatises, which were written when Richard was over forty years of age and near the end of his life; helped by the judiciously selective account of his career given in the Office of St. Richard Hermit, prepared towards the end of the fourteenth century when his canoniza-

[1] *The 'Incendium Amoris' of Richard Rolle of Hampole.* Edited by Margaret Deanesly. (Manchester University Press, 1915.)

[2] *Writings ascribed to Richard Rolle Hermit of Hampole and Materials for his Biography.* By Hope Emily Allen. (Oxford University Press, 1927.) And *English Writings of Richard Rolle Hermit of Hampole.* Edited by Hope Emily Allen. (Oxford University Press, 1931.)

tion was hoped for.[1] We are now able for the first time to place works and legends in their proper context, and trace through them the story of a soul which had endured many vicissitudes before achieving the degree of spiritual maturity which is revealed in Rolle's latest works.

Few pursuits are more fascinating than the study of those stages through which spiritual genius passes, and the gradual transmutation of character which is effected by the discipline of the interior life. It is such a study of Rolle's evolution which Miss Allen has at last made possible for us, and which constitutes for many readers the chief interest of her large and learned book. Did we rely on the 'Office' alone, we should be obliged to regard Rolle as an extreme example of precocious holiness, who abandoned the world as a lad of eighteen, was rapidly raised to the heights of sanctity, and thereafter led the conventional life of a hermit-saint; partly a solitary contemplative, partly a wandering evangelist and trainer of souls. We should know nothing of that tempestuous individualism, those conflicts with ecclesiastical authority and outspoken criticisms of the religious orders, those arrogant claims to the possession of sainthood, which were marked characteristics of his early years. Thus we should lose all the force and interest of the contrast between the egoistic fervour and the self-oblivious spirituality of his earlier and his later works, showing the slow victory of *Anima* over an *Animus* of peculiar vigour and power.

[1] *The Officium and Miracula of Richard Rolle of Hampole.* Edited by R. M. Woolley, D.D. (S.P.C.K., London, 1919.)

All this and much more Miss Allen's researches have revealed to us, providing an invaluable mass of materials on which all future students will be able to work. Work, however, is the right word to use in describing the reader's relation with so large and technical a treatise; and a few signposts may not come amiss to those inclined for the encounter. I propose therefore to summarize what appear to me the chief conclusions to be drawn from her book as to Richard's inner history and status as a mystic.

Miss Allen gives good reason for supposing that the date, 1290, usually given for Rolle's birth is too early. He was probably born about 1300 in the Pickering district of Yorkshire; and almost certainly died in the great plague year of 1349. We must therefore remember that the expressions 'early' and 'late' have in reference to his work a limited significance. He died in the prime of life, and his writings are those of youth and of maturity. We must expect from him nothing of that deep reflection, that geniality, tranquillity and peace, which seem the special gifts of old age to the contemplative. Rolle shows with disarming candour the raw material of sanctity, and lets us discern something of the process whereby that raw material was subdued to the purposes of God; but the curtain falls before the last act in the great drama of the soul's transfiguration has been reached.

We must suppose that Richard was a promising boy, since he was sent to Oxford—probably at thirteen, the normal age—and remained there four years. His known career begins at the end of this period ; with the well-known scene, so picturesquely described in the ' Office ', of his adoption of a hermit's career, and the conversion of two of his sister's frocks into a habit. Here it is perhaps worth while to remark on the intimate connexion in this country between mysticism and the eremitic life. English mysticism begins, historically, in the great religious revival of the twelfth century, which produced a vigorous cult of the solitary life ; and has its earliest literary masterpiece in the *Ancren Riwle*. Though the heroic austerity of the first Cistercians attracted many fervent souls, spiritual enthusiasm seems on the whole to have chosen the ' singular ' path to perfection more often than that which was offered by the monastic orders. When Rolle appeared, at the opening of that which was destined to be the golden age of English mysticism, the north had many memories of hermit saints, and a continuous tradition of ' singular living ' ; and in judging his adoption of this life, and what it meant to him, we should remember his almost certain knowledge of the path his spiritual ancestors had trod, and the romantic appeal of the legends which had gathered round their names. It may have been due to his example and prestige that a revival of the eremitic life took place in the fourteenth century ; since he complains in the *Melum* that whereas in ancient days many of the more perfect went out from the monasteries to dwell in solitary places, now none do this ' and thus without doubt they lack the visitation of angels '.

This conviction of the superior character of the solitary life never left Rolle ; and the new current of mysticism which he started in England maintained a close connexion with the anchoretic ideal. In the next generation both *The Scale of Perfection* and *The Cloud of Unknowing* were written for recluses: and witness by the loftiness of their counsels to the spiritual maturity of those to whom they were addressed. Julian of Norwich, perhaps the greatest of the English mystics, was an anchoress. Thus, if at the beginning Rolle's 'singular purpose' seems inspired by a boyish love of the romantic and picturesque, a determination to cut a striking figure in the religious world, and a rather unpleasing contempt of ordinary ways, the method is well within the lines of contemporary piety. The word hermit covered in his day a wide variety of vocations, from the extreme ascetic to the pious vagabond; and could even include the comfortable agricultural life of the hermit William of Dalby, whom Edward II confirmed in his right of pasturage for two cows.

A comparison of the notices given in the 'Office' with Rolle's earliest writings, and the confessional passages in his later work, help us to reconstruct the first phase in his development. These sources present him as a brilliant, ardently religious boy; impetuous, self-opinionated, full of reforming zeal and strong in a sense of his own vocation. It was probably in the parish church of Pickering that he preached his first sermon, as described in the 'Office'; and attracted the attention of the wife of John de Dalton, the Constable of Pickering Castle. For the next three years he seems to have occupied—if one may say so with respect—the position of tame hermit in the Dalton establishment; living in a room or cell where he could be visited, and exhibited by his patrons to their guests. It apparently opened upon the farm-yard, and the noise of the carters, the flies and the summer heat provided ample opportunity for the exercise of patience. The physical and mental discomforts of this situation for a young, self-occupied and somewhat irritable contemplative, need no emphasis; and Richard, whose temperament did not incline him to silent endurance, described them vigorously in later life. The picture which is given in the 'Office', of the youthful recluse steadily continuing his writing, whilst he emitted (dare we say automatically?) the pious remarks expected by his visitors, has its pathetic as well as its edifying side.

Perhaps because Richard turned out less sensational than he had hoped, perhaps because his impassioned denunciations of wealth and worldliness took on too personal a tone, John de Dalton seems to have tired of his hermit; 'they changed towards me who were accustomed to minister to me', and bad food and neglect were added to the other disadvantages of his position. The eager brilliant boy who had decided on an impulse for 'singular living' was beginning to learn something of its cost. If we regard the descriptions of spiritual development in Rolle's later works as evidence of his own experience—and in so subjective a writer it is probably safe to do this—we shall infer that the period of residence at Pickering was a time of severe and increasing self-discipline. Apparently without help—for it is a peculiarity of his story that he seems to have had no master in the spiritual life—he was undergoing his novitiate: fighting temptations, and coming into contact with the stern realities of the ascetic vocation.

His first experience of spiritual joy, when in his own words 'the heavenly door' opened and revealed to the eyes of his heart the countenance he loved, occurred nearly three years after his conversion. We shall perhaps be correct in interpreting this as his introduction into the world of mental prayer, and dedication to that beautiful type of Christocentric fervour which was expressed by the medieval cult of the Holy Name, and remained to the end of his life his characteristic devotion. For there is hardly a trace in Rolle of that devouring passion for the transcendent Godhead 'in Himself and for Himself alone' so magnificently set forth by the writer of *The Cloud of Unknowing* and his school. For Richard 'the path to the Divinity lay through the Humanity'. Hence it is that the devotion to the Holy Name of Jesus, which sprang up in Western Europe in the later Middle Ages and was no doubt fostered by Franciscan influence, is central for an understanding of his mysticism and colours all his work. It is the very substance of his religion; the recurrent refrain of his most ecstatic outpourings, the dominant theme of his poems.

Jesu that me life has lent, into thy love me bring.
Take to thee all my intent, that thou be my yearning.
Woe from me away were went, and come were my coveting
If that my soul had heard and hent the song of thy loving.

In this characteristic verse from one of his loveliest lyrics [1] we surely detect the direct influence of *Jesu*

[1] 'A Song of the Love of Jesus.' (*English Writings*, p. 43.) I have modernized the spelling.

dulcis memoria as well as of the whole world of religious feeling of which it was born; and many pages of the *Incendium*, on the whole the most characteristic of his writings, read like a lover's commentary upon the Rosy Sequence. Had we to choose one sentence in which his spirituality is most fully expressed, it would probably be the famous declaration 'My heart thou hast bound in love of thy Name, and now I cannot but sing it!'

The 'heavenly door', he says, remained open for a year: that period of spiritual light and consolation which is often experienced by beginners in the contemplative life. We must probably place within this his departure from the Daltons' protection in search of a more tranquil and truly solitary cell; and also the composition of his earliest known work *Judica me*. This exhortation to unworldly life has no mystical characters; but is already marked by his intense interest in the reform of the clergy, and almost Franciscan passion for evangelical poverty.

Until recently it was assumed that the rest of Rolle's life was spent as a wandering hermit and preacher in the Yorkshire dales. But Miss Allen, exploring the vast and chaotic *Melum Contemplativorum*, which she is probably the first person to have read, has discovered evidence that Rolle's early life was more eventful than had been supposed. It now appears that his independent habits, and ruthless criticisms not only of the secular clergy but of the monks, brought him into violent conflict with the local ecclesiastical authorities—probably the great Cistercian Abbots of Rievaulx and Byland. The constant references in his 'Canticles' to monastic shortcomings, and to disputes with the professed religious, show that these denunciations formed a large element in his early preaching; for he was at this stage at least as much reformer as contemplative, devoured by the mystic's longing to bring all outward religion into conformity with his inner light. All this doubtless made him very popular with the laity, among whom dislike of the monasteries was growing up; but it was equally certain to rouse hostility in the great Cistercian houses of the North Riding, whose inhabitants were unlikely to enjoy having at their doors an eloquent young critic with an unsparing tongue, unblushing self-confidence, and rigidly ascetic ideals. Thus Rolle's situation presently became so dangerous that his friends were obliged to hide him from his persecutors: a fact which harmonizes with the possibility—likely enough on other grounds—that he spent at this period some time at the University of Paris.

A MS. history of the Sorbonne, compiled from earlier sources and now in the library of the Arsenal, gives Richardus de Hampole as having been admitted about 1320 and again as resident in 1326. Miss Allen, who discusses these entries in detail, points out that though not conclusive they deserve consideration, and are consistent with the rest of our biographical material. They give an explanation of Rolle's extensive theological knowledge, as shown particularly in his erudite Latin and English psalters; knowledge which is otherwise very difficult to account for. A yet more important consequence is that, if true, they establish direct connexion between the English school of which Rolle was the founder, and the mystical tradition of Western Europe. The great Dominican, Meister Eckhart, who had been in Paris in 1302 and 1311, was still living, and at the height of his reputation. It is at least probable that his Latin works were known in the Paris schools. His pupils Suso and Tauler were Rolle's contemporaries. He could hardly avoid some knowledge of their doctrine, though hardly a trace of its influence can be found in his work. The great Franciscan Spirituals, with whom he has far more temperamental kinship, were now dead. But memories of their teaching, and of the Joachist prophecies that inspired it, lingered both in France and Italy; to form part of that strong current setting towards a mystical and evangelical Christianity, which was felt both inside and outside the Church. There would then be much in the religious atmosphere of Paris to encourage Rolle in his religious individualism, his anti-clerical bias, and his reforming zeal.

If he indeed took refuge in Paris when the situation in Yorkshire became acute, perhaps it was there that he experienced the mystical states he calls 'Heat, Sweetness, and Song'; a triad, perpetually recurring in his writings, to which as time passed he gave more and deeper meaning. As Julian of Norwich tells us that her 'revelations' were all given in a five-hours' trance, and sufficed for a lifetime of meditation, so Rolle's ecstatic experience seems to have been condensed into two vivid illuminations, nine months apart. Looking back on these twenty years later, the impression was yet so strong that he could say he then achieved 'the highest degree of the love of Christ he was able to reach'. Such cases remind us how small a space abnormal phenomena actually occupy in the lives of the great mystics. Their real credentials abide, not in these peculiar and transitory experiences of the supernatural, but in the completeness of their surrender to the supernatural: their faithful correspondence to that which is revealed. Rolle's life is a particularly instructive example of this distinction between the abrupt and 'given' character of the mystical experience and the slow travail of the mystical life; the fact that 'knowledge comes but wisdom lingers' in the world of spirit as well as in the world of sense. Either in Paris or elsewhere, nearly a year after those beginnings of sensible devotion which he calls the 'opening of the door', he was sitting in a chapel 'finding great delight in the sweetness of prayer'—a significant and revealing phrase—when suddenly he felt within 'an unwonted and pleasant heat'. Lest any should suppose this to be a metaphor for a special degree of fervour, he describes here and elsewhere his amazement as the 'burning of his soul burst up', and how he even felt his breast to see whether this heat was of physical origin.

In the presence of such events, the modern critic at once proceeds to the utterance of those comfortable words 'psycho-physical automatism' and feels that no more need be said. But this reference does not really dispose of the subject, or its interest. The comparative study of mysticism shows that the term 'fire of love' or its equivalent carries a precise meaning for those who use it; and that the experience it implies cannot entirely be accounted for in terms of suggestion. Though we need not be afraid to acknowledge that the form taken by religious experience is always influenced by traditional symbols, Miss Allen's statement that what Rolle now 'felt sensuously he first learned academically' hardly covers the facts. When Pascal could find no better words than 'fire' and 'joy' to describe his overwhelming revelation of reality, we may surely suppose here some likeness to Rolle's great experience; and perhaps it is again the same mysterious phenomenon, which a modern contemplative describes when she says of her own initiation into Divine love,

> J'ai été saisie, possédée par une flamme intérieure, dont rien ne m'avait donné l'idée, des *vagues de feu* se succédant pendant près de deux heures.[1]

In such experiences as these, sense and spirit cooperate. Though the mechanism may be docile to psychological analysis, an element is present with which psychology cannot deal. So too with the final form taken by Rolle's intuition of reality; the *Canor* or Song of Joy which came to him nine months after the Heat. As those whose apprehension of spiritual realities takes a visionary form, declare that they are shown a light, a colour, and a loveliness which exceed anything that the world of the senses can give; so the 'heavenly melody' which made him 'miraculous in mind through music' so far exceeded the harmonies heard with the ear of the senses, that they created in him an absolute distaste for 'all mundane melody, all music made with instruments'—even for the liturgical chants of the Church.

Mr. Dundas Harford, in his edition of *The Mending of Life*, pointed out the striking parallel between Rolle's

[1] *Madeleine Sémer Convertie et Mystique 1874–1921*, p. 71.

experience of 'celestial sound' and that of St. Chad, as given by Bede. St. Chad, a week before his death, heard in his oratory 'a sweet sound of singing and rejoicing descend from heaven to earth . . . and return to heaven with unspeakable sweetness'; and when we remember the neighbourhood of Rolle's first cell to Lastingham, with its memories of the saint, we cannot dismiss the probability that this story was known and dear to him. Nevertheless that 'ghostly song' which, more than anything else, gives us the peculiar temper of his spirituality, cannot be disposed of as due to unconscious memory alone. It is better understood as the special form under which the celestial beauty impinging on our life was apprehended by his music-loving soul: a form doubtless suggested by current religious symbols, and perhaps connected with the

Jubilo del core
Che fai cantar d'amore—

described by Jacopone da Todi (whose poems were known in Paris by Rolle's day) and other mystics. The *Jubilus*, which often appears in mystical literature, was not a general term for unbridled emotionalism. It was the name of a recognized type of spiritual experience. 'The *Jubilus*', says Ruysbroeck, 'hath no words, and no man knoweth it save him who hath conceived it in his heart . . . thence cometh joyfulness, and the same is a heartfelt love and a *burning* of devotion . . . and he who conceiveth this *sweetness*, and yet seeketh therein his own delight without thanking and praising God therefore, is utterly at fault.'

Here then, in a mystic of all others most foreign to his temperament, we find associated Rolle's triad of Song, Heat, Sweetness. Yet how different is the status given to them by the English and the Flemish contemplative. 'This heavenly song of the love of God which is called *Jubilus*', says Rolle in one of his latest works, 'is the end of perfect prayer and of the highest devotion that may be here.' 'The *Jubilus*', says Ruysbroeck, 'is the first and *lowest* mode whereby God inwardly declares Himself in the Contemplative Life'; and here he would certainly be supported by all the great masters of prayer. This comparison suggests that Rolle's status as a mystic has been over-estimated; and that the extreme beauty of his Christo-centric rhapsodies and 'elevations' has blinded us to the fact that they mostly belong to the literature of sensible devotion. It is certain that for him, the emotional experiences which he translated as *Calor, Dulcor* and *Canor* remained the *ne plus ultra* of spirituality. 'Here', he says in the *Melum*, 'is shown the highest grade of the Love of God; for by great Heat and divinely given Sweetness the most holy lover flows into Song, and now (as if set in heaven) is all bathed in harmony.'[1] So in the touching prayer with which the *Incendium* ends; the prayer of maturity looking wistfully back at the fervours of youth:

> Jhesu bone, redde mihi organum celicum canticum angelorum, ut in hoc rapiar laudes tuas jugitur modulari; quod dedisti nescienti et non cognoscenti, nunc experto et petenti retribue! . . . O bone Jhesu, ligasti cor meum in cogitacione nominis tui, et illud jam non canere non valeo.[2]

[1] *English Writings*, p. 46. [2] *Incendium Amoris*, p. 278.

Though in later years the emotional vehemence of his nature was somewhat disciplined and purified, still the 'delight that passes all wit and feeling' remained for him the essence of religious experience. Not only so, but these consolations seemed to him to guarantee his own sanctity; a point on which he displays a disconcerting assurance. This is placed beyond doubt by the many personal passages of the *Melum*, a work aptly described by Miss Allen as a monument of egocentric enthusiasm. In it Rolle, now aged about twenty-seven, declares that he has already reached 'the eminence of sanctity'. Its theme, 'the glory and perfection of the saints', is frankly treated from the personal angle; and the contrast between the holiness of the recluse and the shortcomings of the clergy is drawn with more vigour than charity. All this raises the serious psychological problem of harmonizing the dispositions revealed in the *Melum*, first with those which we might expect to follow a real 'opening of the heavenly door', and secondly with the devotional beauty of Rolle's latest works, and his enormous spiritual influence on his contemporaries and successors. And this might lead, did time and space allow, to a further study of the degrees in which genius and character co-operate in the works of the mystics. We are hindered by lack of material from any detailed treatment of the later stages of his development; but at least on the analogy of the lives of other contemplatives, we may expect that the emotional expansion and vivid joys of his first period would be followed by a time of difficulty and struggle proportioned to the intensity of the consolations that had preceded it. Many hints in the *Melum* suggest this, and perhaps give us a clue to the disciplines which at last transformed an impulsive religious individualist into a true saint and father of souls.

Rolle's movements between his twenty-third and fortieth year—except for the possible sojourn in Paris—are not exactly known. He was much in Richmondshire, and sometimes at Hampole near Doncaster; where he was friend and adviser of the nuns. Probably, like the Franciscan Spirituals, he alternated periods of seclusion with wanderings from place to place; for he combined the instincts of the reforming prophet with those of the poet, scholar and recluse. His great Scripture commentaries, the fruits of much intellectual labour and research, but saturated in his own romantic spirituality, suggest that by the time of their composition he possessed readers and disciples of the educated class, to whom these writings were addressed. His last years are specially connected with one of these, Margaret Kirkby, the St. Clare of this imperfect English Francis. She was a nun of Hampole, who became under his influence an anchoress; and his chief vernacular work, *The Form of Living*, was written in 1348 for her enclosure. It is perhaps an epitome of his own experience that he gives her when he says:

A man or woman that is ordained to contemplative life, first God inspires them to forsake this world, and all the vanity and the covetise and the vile lust thereof. Sithen He leads them by their own, and speaks to their heart; and as the prophet says, He gives them at suck the sweetness of the beginning of love. . . . Sithen when they have suffered many temptations, and foul noyes of thoughts that are idle, and of vanities that will cumber them that cannot destroy them, are passing away, He makes them gather together their heart and fasten only in Him ; and opens to the eye of their souls the gates of heaven, so that ilk eye may look into heaven ; and then the fire of love verily ligges in their heart and burns therein and makes it clean of all earthly filth, and sithen forward and they are contemplative men, and ravished in love.

If we are asked to define the outstanding characteristics of Rolle's mysticism, we must put first that impassioned devotion to the Holy Name, which runs through all his writings and inspires all his rhapsodies. Here it is that the contrast is strongest between the English school descending from him, and the contemporary movement in Germany and Flanders, with its definitely theocentric bias. Rolle shows no trace of the influence of the Dionysian writings ; though a theologian of his standing, well acquainted with the Victorines and other standard authorities, can hardly have been ignorant of them. In the opposite direction, he shares the curiously marked aloofness of all the English medieval mystics from Eucharistic devotion and references. An exacting ethical standard, and close contact with the homely realities of human life, give to his doctrine a bracing character ; but on the whole his outlook is that of the lover, musician and poet. Like the angels in Mason's great hymn, he 'sings because he sees the Sun'; contemplation is for him an 'inshed melody', and seems to have been closely connected with lyrical expression. As a teacher of the spiritual life we must consider him inferior to the wise and gentle Hilton ; as a religious genius, to Julian of Norwich. Yet he did a greater work for mystical religion in England than either of these. By the very fervour of his delight in God, by his convinced declaration that there is ' nought merrier than grace of contemplation ', he re-kindled the languid fires of divine love, and restored to its primacy the supernatural gift of Joy.

WALTER HILTON

WALTER HILTON of Thurgarton, the author of that great spiritual classic *The Scale of Perfection*, is commonly reckoned among the English medieval mystics; that small yet strangely varied group of God-intoxicated souls. If religious realism, a perpetual pointing on toward God, be the mark of a mystic, then he has every right to that name; but I think he is best understood as a great teaching saint. He was surely that before all else; and would prefer, I think, to be loved and remembered above all else for his careful, exact, untiring instruction of individual souls in their ascent to God. His sanctity is assured to us not by his exhibition of startling and difficult virtues, or by outwardly heroic acts—still less by any of the extraordinary phenomena, ecstasies and visions which are too often regarded as the marks of the mystical saint—but for a far more Christian, more truly supernatural reason; by the continuously life-giving power of his works. He is one of those hidden figures, those quiet and secret friends of God, who have never failed the Church; and through whom Christ's gift of more abundant life reaches the world, and enters those souls that are ready to receive it. Thus we might well regard him as the patron saint of all those who are called to work in obscurity for the increase of that supernatural life in other souls: the pastoral vocation in its most intense form. This hiddenness, this self-effacement, and this immortality of influence, he shares with his probable contemporary the author of *The Cloud of Unknowing*, and with the writer of *The Imitation of Christ.* All these were content—as indeed the greatest Christians commonly are content—to work in and for a few souls; and just because they have been so content, have thus acquired an enduring and ever-widening influence.

For great spiritual work is usually quiet, deep and hidden; unconcerned with publicity. As the deepest teachings of Christ were first given to a small community, a little flock, and only through them spread gradually to the world; so this method is employed again and again by those teaching saints, whose vocation it is to deepen and expand our human knowledge of the supernatural life. That knowledge is not spread by sermons to big congregations. It oozes out drop by drop from hearts that have been transformed in love: and is generally found, when tracked to its source, to arise from the hidden sober life of consecration and prayer led by one devoted soul. Of this truth Walter Hilton is one of the greatest examples. His life is completely hidden from us except at one point, where it emerges to teach and help other men. The three undoubted works of his which we possess are all what would now be called letters of direction of an elaborate kind. He even thought it worth while to write a whole book for the purpose of educating one special soul; for *The Scale of Perfection*, the work by which he is best known, is really a complete guide-book to the spiritual life written in the vernacular for the use of the particular anchoress to whom it is addressed. It is not easy for us, bewildered by the wealth of spiritual literature which is provided for us, to realize what it meant to simple men and women who knew themselves called to the interior life, when for the first time a guide to its mysteries was put into their hands, written in the language of everyday life. As regards the *Scale* there is plenty of internal evidence to prove that this is the literal truth about its origin, and not a mere literary device; though it was quickly copied and circulated, and became what I suppose we should now call a success.

Indeed, Hilton is not alone in thus feeling that it was abundantly worth while to take this or any other amount of trouble in order to further the sanctification of one individual committed to his care: a conviction which is the mark of the great director of souls, the assistant shepherd who really knows his sheep by name, and is too devoted to the needs of the one, to care about the appreciative bleats of the ninety-nine. The Middle Ages give us many examples of this lovely grace: some of the greatest books of Ruysbroeck, for instance, were thus written for the use of a single person, and Hilton's own English contemporary, the unknown writer of *The Cloud of Unknowing*, seems always to have addressed his works to individuals who had demanded his advice. And perhaps it is just because they thus give their treasures so freely, simply, and humbly to those who want them, to the souls next to them, and do not worry about big movements, or messages to the whole world, that the expansion of their influence still goes quietly on.

Apart from these writings of his, all composed with a practical intention for the use of the special persons who needed them, we know almost nothing about Walter Hilton's career, personality, and spiritual experience. He lives for us as the author of one book of massive spirituality and massive common sense: not as an ecstatic, not as a contemplative—though he may have been both—but as a devoted father of souls. A persistent tradition, which is supported by the earliest extant manuscripts of his works, asserts that he lived, wrote, and probably died and was buried as an Augustinian Canon of the Priory of Thurgarton, in Nottinghamshire. We suppose that he was born some time during the first half of the fourteenth century; for it is practically certain that he died in 1396. There is no real evidence that he was ever the Prior of Thurgarton, although this position is sometimes claimed for him. In fact, as the list of fourteenth-century Priors is extant and practically complete, we may almost say with certainty that he never did fill that office; and it seems much more consistent with the character which his work reveals to us that he should have preferred to remain in the background of the community life, undistracted by the many practical duties—including a considerable share in the local government of the district—which had to be fulfilled by the Superior of such a great house as Thurgarton was in his day. He would have been far more fitly occupied with that direction of souls for which he was plainly possessed of peculiar genius ; and with the living out of the exacting interior life which this vocation demands. Pastoral work, theological study and education, were the three chief forms of service to which the Austin Canons were called ; and these were enough to give Hilton the opportunities for full use of his special gifts.

The three works by which we now know Hilton —that is, *The Scale of Perfection*, the beautiful little tract called *The Song of the Angels*, and the *Letter to a Devout Man*—entitle him to high rank among the great English spiritual writers of the fourteenth century ; for I suppose we must agree that Richard Rolle of Hampole, the author of *The Cloud of Unknowing*, and Dame Julian of Norwich represent with him the highest points reached by English medieval spirituality. And of those four, Hilton, who has been by far the most widely and persistently influential, is one of the two who tell us least about themselves ; who show in their work the supreme Christian grace of a complete self-forgetfulness. He and the author of *The Cloud of Unknowing*, rival one another in the perfection of their anonymity, their avoidance of the confessional point of view. Nor, I think, is this anonymity, this avoidance, an attitude which they have deliberately chosen and maintained. Were this so, its perfect ease and graciousness would be impaired. It happens quite naturally and spontaneously, because their supreme interest is in the cherishing and teaching of other souls, in making supernatural personalities ; and not in talking about their own personalities, which are simply left on one side. And they prove to us their lofty supernatural status, by the perfection with which they thus obliterate themselves.

So I think that in considering Hilton's work, the first thing that comes home to us is the way in which, from one quiet man, living in a remote corner of the country, there came out a stream of spiritual culture that has affected ever since the eternal interests of a multitude of souls. And next, that this stream of spiritual culture originates in the patient, skilled, and devoted work done by that one quiet soul for another soul. And thirdly, that this light-giving power depended on and emerged from a hidden life of prayer, almost as complete in its self-effacement as is its Pattern, the hidden life of Christ Himself; a life which claims for itself no special quality or special insight, which refuses even to acknowledge that a personal spiritual experience lies behind its realistic declarations. In these facts taken together, we have surely a great demonstration of the immensity and endurance of the supernatural power which a complete humility is able to release.

We turn, then, from contemplation of this hidden life to the chief book in which Hilton's spirit lives and acts: *The Scale of Perfection.* Even in his lifetime, manuscripts of it seem to have been widely distributed. Before the end of the fourteenth century it had been translated into Latin, and in that form its influence spread on the Continent; and by the middle of the fifteenth it was more read in this country than any other English devotional book. It was printed in 1494, an honour conferred on very few spiritual works; and when we come down to the seventeenth century we find it well known and loved by all who care for the interior life.

In its complete form, the *Scale* consists of two distinct parts each in itself complete. They appear to have been written separately at different periods. Part I exists alone in many MS. versions, and was evidently circulated for some time as a separate work: being considered, as time has proved it to be, a suitable manual for the use of all earnest Christians desiring to follow the 'ordinary ways' of the interior life. It deals with the soul's preparation for the supernatural life of contemplative love, and the first degrees of prayer; its teaching is mainly psychological and ascetic. The second part deals with the soul's development within that life: its teaching is mainly contemplative and mystical. Thus each part assumes a very different status in the person who is addressed; and I do not think it too much to say that each is the fruit of a different stage in Hilton's own development.

The *Scale* is not perhaps, at first sight, the sort of book which many people expect a mystic to produce. It is downright, practical, homely, and realistic. In its first part especially, it embodies much of the ordinary routine teaching of Catholic Christianity. It depends on and perpetually quotes Holy Scripture; here showing perhaps the influence of that determined Bible-Christian Richard Rolle. It keeps very close to human nature's common ways. It dwells quite as much on homely things as lofty things. Yet few books, when we come to understand it, enter more deeply or treat more exactly the essential business of the spiritual life; that is to say, that purification, re-ordering, and transforming of our imperfect personality, which makes it fit for the union with God which is the goal of our spiritual growth—the making of that ' new creature ' which St. Paul felt a real Christian must be. Von Hügel has somewhere spoken of ' the mysterious paradox which pervades all true life ; and which shows us the human soul as self-active in proportion to God's action within it '. That phrase might serve as a fitting introduction to Hilton's great book ; for he is one of the very best teachers of that double movement of docility and initiative—the real and powerful working of the holy energy we call grace, and yet the absolute need of a vigorous use of our own will—through which human personality is transformed and sanctified. Were his work re-written in the psychological language of the present day, its literary quality would certainly be reduced. But we should then perhaps realize better how profound and how exact was his understanding of our many-levelled human nature, its cravings and its needs.

The whole of Hilton's teaching is based on the two great realities with which all religion is concerned : the perfect and rich reality of God, and the partial and derived reality of the soul, and the essential correspondence existing between them. In the first part of the *Scale*, the centre of the picture is occupied by the natural or, as he prefers to say, the ' unreformed ' man or woman. Perhaps it is easier for us to use here the word ' untransformed '. We are to understand by this term the soul whose latent spiritual quality has been obscured, overlaid by the image of sin ; but who desires and is capable of transformation into the spiritual man, or 'reformed image'. This transformation, this restoration of human personality to what it ought to be, takes in Christian experience two distinct forms. The average good man—and also the soul destined to fullness of spiritual life whilst still in its earlier stages—is 'reformed in faith' by a faithful effort to co-operate with God, and lead the Christian life. But these have no conscious experience of a fundamental change in their world and their life; as Rolle would say, of 'the opening of the heavenly door'. Only those who go further—and to them the Second Book of the *Scale* is addressed—are reformed in 'feeling' as well as in 'faith'; achieving an experimental knowledge of God's Presence, and of His union with the soul in love. And it is only in so far as she uses her exceptional devotional opportunities for that most lofty and most practical end, that the anchoress for whom Hilton writes is justified in his sight in her special way of living. She is released from the complications of active life and human society only in order that the inward work may be more vigorously and thoroughly done.

The opening phrase of the book at once sets the note of Hilton's teaching; its actuality, its determined insistence on facts :

> Hold thou content and stand steadfastly, travailling busily with all the mights of thy soul for to fulfil in soothfastness of good living the state which thou hast taken in likeness and in seeming. . . . For wit thou well, a bodily turning to God without the heart following is but a figuring and likeness of virtues and no soothfastness.

Look, he says in effect, at the facts. What is it that you have promised to do? You have promised—not merely for your own soul's sake but as a servant of the Church—to live the contemplative life. This is a tremendous undertaking, not to be accomplished merely by shutting yourself up and performing devotional exercises.

Contemplative life lieth in perfect love and charity felt inwardly, by ghostly virtues, and by soothfast knowing and sight of God and ghostly things.

Such perfect love, such steady attention to Eternity, is not to be had at small cost.

Now then [he says to her in his bracing way] since it is so that thy state asketh for to be contemplative, for that is the end and the intent of thine enclosing, that thou mightest more freely and entirely give thee to ghostly occupation: then behoveth thee for to be right busy night and day with travail of body and of spirit, for to come to that life as near as thou mightest, by such means as thou hopest were best unto thee.

He then proceeds, bit by bit, to discuss the means, and the way in which she may use them; with the penetrating exactitude of a psychologist, and the homely common sense of an experienced father of souls. These means of becoming more spiritual can be classed under three heads. First, knowledge of self over against God: a clear view of our nothingness, fragility, and dependence. Next, the inward seeking of Christ in contemplation and prayer, a process which is at first 'travaillous but the finding is blissful'. Last, the discovery and mortifying of sin—that element in human nature which is hostile to God—at its very source. These are quite enough to keep the average soul fairly busy. We feel that Hilton would have agreed with St. Teresa, in summing up the whole interior life as 'work, suffering, and love'.

Thus, in the technical language of mysticism, we might say that Hilton treats first and fully of the way of purgation; and only after this has been completely charted goes on to those mystical experiences which mark the progress of the purified and expanded soul towards perfect union with God. But he does not deal very much in this technical language. He has his own symbolism, frequently Biblical and always homely and direct, in which he treats of that long, hard, and costly work throughout which Divine grace and man's will must co-operate, ever rising and falling together, if the soul is ever to reach its spiritual goal; that is to say, the point where no discord exists between the Creator and the created spirit. It is remarkable how free from rigid and doctrinaire notions, how close to psychological truth, is Hilton's treatment of this subject. 'Man', he says—here of course following St. Augustine, that prince of psychologists —'is naught else but his thoughts and his loves'; and freedom consists in a certain limited power of directing those thoughts and those loves. Thus the true character of his desires and intentions, the direction of his emotional drive, is all-important for man's spiritual destiny. One chief point in self-knowledge is the discovery of our real centre of interest; and the test proposed still retains its validity—

If thou wilt wit what thou lovest, look whereupon thou thinkest; for where thy love is there is the eye, and where thy liking is, there is most the heart thinking. If thou love mickle God, thee liketh for to think mickle of Him ; and if thou love little, then little thou thinkest of Him.

Hilton feels with St. Augustine, whom he frequently quotes without acknowledgement, that it is the pull of these fundamental desires and interests, what we do with them, how we transform and spiritualize them, which is decisive in the life of the soul. The perfection to which each is called, involves the complete dedication of those thoughts and those loves with which it is endowed to God, who is Reality ; and the cost and tension of the supernatural life consists in the drastic process of transmutation through which alone this end can be achieved. Though God is indeed the prime agent in everything which concerns that supernatural life—though, in the deepest sense, He is all and does all too—yet man's obligation of effort, choice, and response begins at the first moment and continues all the time. It is largely by the exercise of this free though limited will and choice, its complete unification and concentration on one point, that he grows up from a narrow selfhood into a creature with a capacity for God.

An whole and a stable intention, that is for to say, an whole will and a desire *only* for to please God,

is the first necessity. A solid realization of what the soul truly wants and what it means to do, a deliberate, costly seeking and attending, is the condition under which He is found. Under the symbolism of the lost piece of silver of the Gospels, Hilton describes the search and the discovery of Christ the Divine Reason hidden within the soul; the vigorous sweeping out of dark corners, and the diligent, painstaking seeking demanded by this episode in its career.

> Thou hast lost Him, but where? Soothly in thine house, that is in thy soul. If thou haddest lost Him out of thine house, that is to say, if thou haddest lost all the reason of thy soul by the first sin, thy soul should never have found Him again; but He left to thee reason, and so He is in thy soul and never shall be lost out of it. Nevertheless thou art never the nearer to Him till thou hast found Him.

He leaves us in no doubt that the spiritual life is a real job and not an agreeable dream. It involves work, indeed drudgery; on the moral level and on the devotional level too. Devotion and moral effort must go hand in hand: one alone is useless. For it is only when sin is seen in the spirit of prayer, and in contrast with the spirit of Christ, that its character is fully perceived and its destruction completely willed.

Only this destruction of sin at the root, this purgation and transformation of the very heart of personality, is, he thinks, ultimately worth while. Anything short of this is a mere scratching of the surface; and however impressive it may be in appearance, does not impress him very much. He observes, with his characteristic love of homely and realistic imagery, that the 'untransformed' human soul is rather like a garden in which there is a foul and stinking pond, with runnels of bad water running out of it in all directions. We may stop up the runnels one by one, thus apparently curing ourselves of separate sinful tendencies —pride, anger, envy, and the rest—but unless the secret root of all these evil dispositions, namely 'a false misruled love unto thyself', has been extirpated, it will merely pay you out for that policy of repression by soaking into the ground and poisoning the whole personality. This is a bit of psychological analysis which we might now express in other terms, but of which few would deny the essential truth. Self-love, he thinks, *must* be destroyed at the root, the only place where it can be attacked with any hope of success; and this is the first and hardest stage in that reforming of the defaced image of the soul, which is to bring it back to the lost likeness of God. It must be done, or at least must seem to us to be done, largely by our own efforts, by a deliberate and patient exercise of will; but this personal struggle is really to be considered as only preparatory to those deeper purifications in which the emphasis is shifted from that which each person must do for himself, to that which God alone can do in the soul.

In the second part of *The Scale of Perfection* it is this Divine action and the disposition in which man can receive it, which is treated as central to the development of the true supernatural or contemplative life. Here loving surrender and confidence take the place of anxious struggle; and the great humbling and pacifying truth of man's nothingness, and the joy and power that come with its acknowledgement, dominate all other aspects of the soul's relation to God. Again and again Hilton brings his pupil back to the one all-embracing declaration 'I am nothing; I have nothing; I desire nothing save Jesu only' —the single reply which the pilgrim to Jerusalem, which is the City of the Love of God, is to make to all who try to frighten him or deflect him from his way. The passage in which he describes the soul's journey to Jerusalem is one of the best known and most beautiful in his works, and curiously anticipates Bunyan's dream.

> Right as a true pilgrim going to Jerusalem leaveth behind him house and land, wife and child, and maketh himself poor and bare from all that he hath, that he might go lightly without letting: right so, if thou wilt be a ghostly pilgrim, thou shalt make thyself naked from all that thou hast, that are both good deeds and bad, and cast them all behind thee; that thou be so poor in thine own feeling that there be nothing of thine own working that thou wilt lean upon restingly, but aye desiring more grace of love, and aye seeking the ghostly presence of Jhesu. And if thou do thus, then shalt thou set in thy heart wholly and fully, that thou wouldest be at Jerusalem and at none other place but there. And that is, thou shalt set in thine heart wholly and fully, that thou wouldest nothing have but the love of Jhesu, and the ghostly sight of Him as He will show Him; for to that only thou art made and bought, and that is thy beginning and thine end, thy joy and thy bliss.

It is a policy of entire consecration, of total concentration on the soul's one end that Hilton asks for: the solemn affirmation of St. Ignatius, 'I come from God, I belong to God, I am destined for God', stated in the gentler terms of Christo-centric love.

In this second part of *The Scale of Perfection* he is of course addressing a pupil far more advanced in the spiritual life than was his ghostly sister when he first undertook her education. The strict ascetic training, and instruction on methods of prayer, which fill the earlier chapters have now done their work; and a larger, deeper, more supple, and more genial method is opened up before us. The emphasis no longer falls on self-improvement and self-discipline; but rather on a free and joyful self-abandonment, the simple yet profound communion of the soul with Christ which is the essence of the life of contemplation as taught by Hilton and his school.

> What thou hast or what thou dost, hold it as nought for to rest in, without the sight and the love of Jhesu. Cast it all behind thee and forget it, that thou might have that that is the best of all.

The recluse who was once told to 'labour and swink busily' at the getting of virtues has profited by her lessons, and is now ready to be taught St. Paul's more excellent way; in which the whole of the business and work of the contemplative life is seen to be comprehended in love.

> This love [says Hilton] is nought else but Jhesu Himself, that for love worketh all this in a man's soul and reformeth it in feeling to His likeness, as I have before said, and somewhat also I shall say. This love bringeth into the soul the fullhead of all virtues, and maketh them all clean and true, soft and easy, and turneth them all into love and into liking; and on what manner wise He doth it, I shall tell thee a little afterward. This love draweth the soul from fleshlihood into ghostliness, from earthly feeling into heavenly savour, and from vain beholding of worldly things into contemplation of ghostly creatures, and of God's privities.

We have now moved away from the instructions suited to beginners, to those appropriate to advanced souls; souls who are really, as Hilton says, reformed in feeling as well as in faith—in other words, who actually *feel* different, and are capable of conscious communion with God. And here we feel too that the mature soul of the author involuntarily discloses some of its own secrets ; which are simply the unchanging secrets of the developed life of prayer, as it is lived by one who is no longer just the faithful servant, but the consciously loving and dependent child of God. Hilton now begins to write with that accent of delighted certitude, of unselfconscious joy which is, of all things in religion, strongest in its missionary appeal. Thus, in the beautiful passage in which he describes the humility and genial indifference which come, not from the vision of self in its horror but from the intimate presence of Christ in His perfection, we can hardly doubt that a personal experience speaks to us across the centuries.

For the heart of a true lover of Jhesu is made so mickle and so large through a little sight of Him and a little feeling of His ghostly love, that all the liking and all the joy of all earth may not suffice for to fill a corner of it. And then seemeth it well that these wretched worldly lovers that are as it were ravished in love of their own worship, and pursue after it for to have it with all the might and the will that they have, they have no savour in this meekness, they are wonder far therefrom. But the lover of Jhesu hath this meekness lastingly, and that not with heaviness and striving for it, but with liking and gladness : the which gladness he hath, not for he forsaketh the worship of the world, for that were a proud meekness that longeth to an hypocrite, but for he hath a sight and a ghostly knowing of soothfastness and of worthiness of Jhesu through the gift of the Holy Ghost.

That reverent sight and that lovely beholding of Jhesu comforteth the soul so wonderfully and beareth it up so mightily and so softly, that it may not like nor fully rest in none earthly joy, nor it will not. He maketh no account whether men blame him or praise him, worship him or despise him as for himself. He setteth it not at heart neither for to be well paid if men despise him, as for more meekness, nor for to be evil paid that men should worship him or praise him. He had liefer for to forget both that one and that other, and only think on Jhesu, and get meekness by that way; and that is mickle the securer way, whoso might come thereto.

For Hilton, then, the science and art of contemplation is simply the science and art of perfect love. He would say with St. Augustine: 'Love, and do what you like'. In the light of his teaching we begin to understand why it was that St. Teresa called such contemplation 'a short cut to perfection',—a phrase that is frequently misunderstood. It is truly a short cut, in so much as it aims at the very heart and centre of the supernatural life; takes the straight way uphill to the City of the Love of God without considering the surface and the gradient, instead of the long and gradual spiral travelled by the non-contemplative soul. It involves such an absorption of the whole human self in its assigned end, which is God, that the centre of interest is changed, and merely self-regarding sins become impossible to it.

Love worketh wisely and softly in a soul where he will, for he slayeth mightily ire and envy and all passions of angriness and melancholy in it, and bringeth into the soul virtues of patience and mildness, peaceability and amity to his even-christian. It is full hard and a great need to a man that standeth only in working of his own reason, for to keep patience, holy rest and softness in heart, and charity to his even-christian if they trouble him unreasonably and do him wrong, that he shall not somewhat do again to them through stirring of ire or of melancholy, either in speaking or in working or in both.

But to a true lover of Jhesu is no great need for to suffer all this; for why, love fighteth for him, and slayeth wonder softly such stirring of wrath and of melancholy, and maketh his soul so easy, so peaceable, so suffering and so godly through the ghostly sight of Jhesu with the feeling of His blessed love, that though he be despised and reproved of other men, or take wrong or harm, shame or villainy, he chargeth it not.

Such an achievement as this means the discovery, not in idea but in literal fact, that the whole of the supernatural life in its utter devotion to the interests of reality, its steadfast movement towards union with God—all that some spiritual writers make so elaborate, so inhuman, and so difficult—every bit of this can be comprehended in the single practice of a self-oblivious love. It means the replacement of all self-occupied spirituality, all scruples and direct struggle with sins, by a simple and total loving adherence to God in Christ. But the soul has a long way to go before it can understand and practise this, in the actual sense in which the great mystics understand it; and, as a fact, the great division between the ascetic and the mystical levels of the life of prayer lies here. The distinction is in the soul's experience and practice of love, its capacity for that gentle and complete renunciation which brought Pascal certitude, joy and peace.

For a soul that hath the gift of love through gracious beholding of Jhesu as I mean, or else if he have it not yet but would have it, he is not busy for to strain himself over his might, as it were by bodily strength, for to have it by bodily fervours and so for to feel of the love of God. But him thinketh that he is right nought, and that he can do right nought of himself; but as it were a dead thing only hanging and borne up by the mercy of God. He seeth well that Jhesu is all and doth all, and therefore asketh he nought else but the gift of His love. For since that the soul seeth that his own love is nought, therefore it would have his love, for that is enough. Therefore prayeth he, and that desireth he, that the love of God would touch him with His blessed light, that he might see a little of Him by His gracious presence, for then should he love Him ; and so by this way cometh the gift of love, that is God, into a soul.

But ' this realization ', says Hilton, ' can only be had for much bodily and ghostly labour going before '. It is not the easy trick offered by the Quietists ; but a gift of God which is the reward of humble and faithful effort, steady discipline and purification. It brings with it a wise suppleness, the gentle acquiescence in the pace and the purpose of God which is the essence of true humility ; and is far more effective than the wild first-hand struggle for personal attainment of those whom he calls ' lovers of God that make themselves for to love God as it were by their own might '.

And so it seemeth that neither grace only without full working of a soul that in it is, nor working alone without grace, bringeth a soul to reforming in feeling ; the which reforming standeth in perfect love and charity. But that one joined to that other, that is grace joined to working, bringeth into a soul the blessed feeling of perfect love, the which grace may not rest fully but on a meek soul, that is full of dread of God.

Full of dread of God : awe, a quality often missed out of those encouraging little books which assure us that religion is so natural and so easy, all breadth and no depth. The great revealers of the mysteries of God have never dared to talk like that.

This second book of the *Scale* is really in its wholeness a treatise on the communion of the soul with

God in Christ. Even a casual reading, much more an intimate acquaintance with it, brings home to us the intensely personal character of medieval devotion; how vividly actual and realistic was its Christocentric orientation, the glow and colour, the depth and gentle intimacy, which are united in its passionate worship of the Holy Name. English mysticism has its origin in that intense devotion to the Person of our Lord, which arose in this country in the twelfth century. And although we cannot deny that Hilton shares with his contemporaries the curious aloofness of the English mystics from the Sacraments, the doctrine of the contemplative life which he develops in this book might well be called the mysticism of the Real Presence.

> How that presence is felt [he says], it may better be known by experience than by any writing; for it is the life and the love, the might and the light, the joy and the rest of a chosen soul. And therefore he that hath soothfastly once felt it, he may not forbear it without pain; he may not undesire it, it is so good in itself and so comfortable. What is more comfortable to a soul here than for to be drawn out through grace from the vile noye of worldly business and filth of desires, and from vain affection of all creatures into rest and softness of ghostly love; privily perceiving the gracious presence of Jhesu, feelably fed with savour of His unseeable blessed face? Soothly nothing, me thinketh. Nothing may make the soul of a lover full merry, but the gracious presence of Jhesu as He can show Him to a clean soul.

FINITE AND INFINITE

A STUDY OF THE PHILOSOPHY OF BARON FRIEDRICH VON HÜGEL

ALL who were privileged to know Baron von Hügel during the last phase of his earthly life retain, in one form or another, two sharply contrasting memories. There is the memory of an immense spiritual transcendency; a personality at once daunting and attractive, an Alpine quality. Those who cherish memories of personal intercourse with him may even be inclined to think first of a volcanic mountain; for he combined a rock-like faith, a massive and lofty intellect, with the incandescent fervour, the hidden fires of an intense interior life. The piercing black eyes which compelled truth and obtained it, the awe and passion which were felt when the Baron uttered the name of his God; these will not be forgotten by any soul which came within his sphere of influence. It has been truly said of those who saw him thus, that they were 'lost in his depth, silenced by his nobility'.

On the other hand, there is the memory of the lovable old man who could be met in the quiet streets of Kensington; making small homely purchases with much deliberation, carrying little paper bags, devoted in the detailed personal care of his little dog. The saint transfigured by his passionate sense of God, the scholar willing to give endless labour to the exact discrimination of some subtle point, was full of unhurried interest in humble people and simple things ; able to enjoy small jokes and homely amusements, and to say with complete simplicity of an ailment or a disappointment, 'Another little humiliation for me—what a good thing ! '

This doubleness, this capacity for moving easily between the homely and the transcendental, the natural and supernatural levels, runs right through von Hügel's life, conversation and teaching ; sometimes appearing with disconcerting effect. In him the thinker and prophet, the contemplative and the father of souls existed in such close union, that we can never understand one of his aspects unless we take some account of all. There is something Augustinian in that massive passion for God which was the heart both of his philosophy and his devotion. Yet the profound and genial understanding of humanity, the homely love of creatures, which was so large a factor in his personal influence as a spiritual teacher, brought him nearer to those great French directors of the Counter-Reformation with whom, too, his sympathy was very deep. And although we must here guard against those tempting simplifications which in religion he held specially hostile to truth, these contrasting aspects of his personality do represent in a striking way that inclusive two-fold attitude towards life eternal and life successive—that double orientation—which was the distinctive mark of the Baron's religious philosophy.

Nor should we regard the homely strain, the gentle geniality of his contacts with the everyday world, as the deliberate condescension of a lofty soul: part, as it were, of that Alpine flora which softens for us the overwhelming majesty of a mountain range. It arose out of the very nature of his conception of Reality. Whether we call that conception, as he did by turns, a critical realism, a limited dualism, or a 'two-step philosophy', its essential character remains the same. It is summed up in the full title which he had intended to give to his unfinished Gifford Lectures: 'The Reality of Finites, and the Reality of God.' In that phrase, von Hügel stated his profound belief, as against all subjective idealism, that the human soul is in real contact with a real world; a world of objects which is truly distinct from ourselves, and possessing an existence in its own right, which transcends and is independent of our awareness. This belief in the genuine 'reality of finites' is of course the foundation-stone of any genuine Christian metaphysic; for the incarnation and self-imparting of the Ultimate through persons and things requires the reality of the incarnating medium, as well as that of the Absolute thus revealed. It involves the deep significance of every level of creation; yet also the fact that this significance is deep and real, just because the significance of God is still more real and deep, and His relation to His world is not a relation of sheer immanence but free, distinct, many-graded, sacramental.

When we say we believe in the Creation, especially when we profess belief in each single soul's free will, we profess the mysterious belief that God has somehow alienated a certain amount of His own power, and given it a relative independence of its own; that He has, as it were, set up (relative but still real) obstacles, limits, friction as it were against Himself. And thus we may well wonder at this mysteriously thin barrier between our poor finite relativity, and the engulfing infinite Absolute, a barrier which is absolutely necessary for us, for though God was and could ever be without us, God is no more God for us, if we cease to be relatively distinct from Him.

Moreover, this two-fold reality is required and guaranteed by the two-fold nature of man. The 'incurably amphibious' character of the human creature, conditioned by the senses yet craving the supersensual, capable of eternal life yet rooted in the time-series, with 'two sets of duties, needs and satisfactions' to the Visible or This World and the Invisible or the Other World: this was a present fact to von Hügel, and he did not hesitate to say that 'this duality precedes and reaches farther than even the duality of good and evil'. Because there was in him something of the poet as well as the prophet, he possessed a penetrating sense of the significance of things; the degree and way in which they are charged with reality, always holding further depths of meaning in reserve for us, and therefore the importance of the very homily in its touching imperfection and appeal. 'I cannot exhaustively know, I cannot adequately define even a daisy'—still less, the full range of any fact concerning the mysterious life of man.

Though our human situation be indeed that of a 'poor little paper boat on the sea of the Infinite' yet God in the very act of creation has given to our fragile existence 'a quite absolute worth'. In all his teaching about life the Baron never forgot the truth, that sanity and lowliness require our reverent acceptance of both levels of our mixed experience ; not an arrogant choice between them. By a succession of images—the mountain and the plain, the edelweiss and alpenrose, the corn-fields and potatoes—he struggled to convey this steady vision of a graded world: the need of nature and grace, sense and spirit, ' the Seen and the Unseen, the Good and the Better or Best '—held together, not set in opposition —for the maturing of man's spirit and full living-out of his peculiar call. ' A polarity, a tension, a friction, a one thing at work in distinctly another thing '—this was for him a fundamental and inevitable character of our spiritual life. Hence the difficult balance he asked in personal religion : ' Variety up to the verge of dissipation : Recollection up to the verge of emptiness ', since

> Only the two movements of World-flight and of World-seeking, of the Civilizing of Spirituality and of the Spiritualizing of Civilization : only This world and That world, each stimulating the other, although in different ways, from different sources and with different ends ; only these two movements together form man's complete supernaturalized Spiritual life.

More and more present to him, was the folly and untruthfulness of any philosophy which sought the eternal by a mere rejection of the temporal ; and the profound need of a creaturely self-immersion in finite loves and duties, if man's thirst for the infinite was to escape arrogance. Here is the origin of the dislike, especially felt in his practical teaching, for any setting in opposition of the beauties and duties of Nature and the attractions of Grace; and the reiterated demand, so disconcerting to the ardent convert, for a careful cultivation of 'non-religious interests'. 'Nature is the expression of the God of Nature, just as Grace is the expression of the God of Grace'—or, in more metaphysical terms, the full reality and overwhelming demand of the Abiding, of Eternal Life, leaves unblemished the lesser demands and realities of the successive world. This truth, the subject of a majestic passage in *The Reality of God*, is given in the most homely terms in one of the 'Letters to a Niece':

> All we do has a double relatedness. It is a link or links of a chain that stretches back to our birth and on to our death. It is part of a long train of cause and effect, of effect and cause . . . but there is also, all the time, another, a far deeper, a most darling and inspiring relation. Here, you have no slow succession, but you have each single act, each single moment joined directly to God—Himself not a chain, but one great simultaneity.

And just because, as he well knew, the human passion for the Universal and Unchanging where it is present so easily becomes intense and over-strained, humble and loving attention to the chain, concern with little things, a sympathetic contact with the homely, become ever more necessary with the deepening of the transcendental sense. 'L'esprit pour vous', said Huvelin to his great pupil, 'c'est un esprit de bénédiction de toute créature': and this was the spirit the Baron strove to cultivate in all his pupils in the interior life.

In the attempt to isolate von Hügel's chief contribution to religious philosophy, and find the key to that ' system ' which we always want our prophets to possess, much stress has been laid on the brilliant analysis of the three elements of religion, in the opening section of *The Mystical Element of Religion*. But when we enter more deeply into his thought, we realize that this analysis—rightly valued, though perhaps somewhat overworked, by apologists ever since—is really no more than a particular application of his governing intuition : that of the many-levelled richness and complexity of life, the organic character of human personality, and the dangerous silliness of simplification when applied to the mysterious scene which confronts our human consciousness, or the more mysterious facts of our inner life.

> Man, where he is, or thinks himself, very learned and unusually penetrating, remains terribly prone to simplify, even where simplicity means a mangling of reality.

It is this humbly realistic outlook which explains von Hügel's deep reverence for concrete things, as the sacramental utterance of God : his doubts about abstractions, as so easily proceeding from the mere cleverness of man.

> Est in re veritas
> Jam non in schemate.

This outlook, profoundly in harmony with Catholic life though not always with Catholic speculation, even included considerable distrust of the claims of ' pure mysticism '. ' The mystic sense flies straight to God, and *thinks* it finds all its delight in Him alone.' But a careful examination always discovers many sensible, institutional, and historical contributions to this supposed ineffable experience; and suggests that the effort to achieve an entirely transcendental religion involves a perilous defiance of the true status and limitations of man. A humble recognition of the reaching-out of the divine to the human, does more for the soul's best interests than any arrogant reaching-out of the human to the divine.

He has told us that his own intellectual evolution began in 'a more or less Idealistic philosophy of an Hegelian type, assumed to be baptizable and indeed baptized'—a metaphysic 'so full of the undoubted activities of the subject, as largely to overlook the distinct reality and the influence of the object'. It ended in a theology, which emphasized the distinctness and prevenience of the known Object; and the conviction, as against all subjectivism, that something 'is really given to us every time we know, and indeed think, at all . . . so that knowledge is never primarily simply a knowledge of our own states, but a knowledge, or at least the seeking for a knowledge', of genuine existents, independent things. Man does look out on a real world greater than all his conceiving. He is not merely face to face with the history of his own mind, and the results of its ingenious workings, but with 'facts of immense length and range in space and time'. And these finite facts, humbly observed and accepted, can open the soul's eyes on that Infinite Fact 'greater than our heart', the Prevenient and Absolute God.

Von Hügel's great intellect came to rest in the conviction that only this realistic view—'a Realism not of Categories or Ideas but of Organisms and Spirits'—

tallied with our experience, whether sensible or spiritual ; and moreover that it was essential to any genuine theism. Once we capitulate to subjectivist habits of mind, we can hardly save God from going into the melting-pot with His world. Here is the metaphysical basis of the generous but discriminating hospitality of his mind to realities of every size and sort ; the interest in geology, the loving delight in plant and animal life, his admiration for the patient, humble labours of a Kepler or a Darwin, and reverence for the exact performance of our normal daily deeds. This sense of the deep but never merely equal significance of everything that *is*, and the danger of all narrowness, one-sidedness, deliberate and excessive concentration on one aspect of experience alone, is summed up in the quotation from St. Augustine which he placed at the beginning of *The Mystical Element.* ' Grant unto man, O God, to perceive in little things the indication, common-seeming though they be, of things both small and great.' On the other hand, this same principle—doubtless reinforced by those experiences which come with the maturing of the Christian inner life—surely lies at the root of that hostility to monism and all ' levelling-down pantheisms ', which grew with the growth of his thought ; so that he could give it as his deepest and perhaps his most controversial conviction, that ' religion has no subtler and yet also no deadlier enemy in the region of the mind, than every and all monism '.

When we come from these considerations to look at von Hügel's achievement, stretching from the long studies which prepared *The Mystical Element* to the last, unfinished work, in which he had hoped to sum up and arrange his final conclusions upon the deepest things of life, we see how this 'two-step reading of Reality' became ever more and more central for him. It is true that *The Reality of God*, as finally published after his death, consists only of such fragments of his projected Gifford Lectures as it was found possible to rescue and arrange: a work of great difficulty, performed with the utmost devotion and skill. Nevertheless, whilst other parts of his writings are richer, warmer, more intimate in tone than this, they all gain by a careful comparison with it. Fortunately the introduction was left in a completed state; and this gives an invaluable clue to the general scheme, and makes it possible to place in correct relationship the isolated passages that succeed it. It shows the great lines on which the Baron had planned this work; which, had he lived to finish it, would have given us something as near to a system as was possible to so richly generous, so unfenced a mind. The very title which he proposed for it, 'The Reality of Finites and the Reality of God', sums up, as we have seen, the central conviction which governs his philosophy; and which became ever more explicit as his mind and soul matured. It means that genuine doubleness of our status and our experience, linked to and learning from the simultaneous and the successive aspects of Reality, which is the clue to the paradox of human life: and because of this the immense importance of the concrete, sensible, finite world of our temporal existence, as the scene within which alone our capacity for the infinite can expand. Therefore a meek creatureliness is the first term of all genuine spirituality, and an excessive abstraction from the here-and-now the most insidious of our ghostly temptations.

Materialism readily appears as the arch-enemy of the spirit; yet, erroneous as materialism is, it very certainly is not the most dangerous of the spirit's enemies. Never to lose the sense that we human beings are body as well as soul, not only here but, in some way and degree difficult or impossible to picture, also in the hereafter, is to keep ourselves sane and balanced.

In this introduction, which is an important document for the right understanding of the Baron's doctrine of knowledge, he laid down three principles which were to control the development of the whole work. They are seen when we examine them, to be various expressions of that realistic outlook, the intense love and reverence for the factual, the objective, which formed one-half of his characteristic reaction to life.

(1) As against all 'theories of development' he declares his method to be based on the patient and loving examination of the Given; that which now is. It is to be analytic rather than genetic: accepting with docility such present facts and achievements of morals, faith or knowledge as we find in the field, without seeking to explain, reduce or discredit them by reference to their primitive origin or embryonic forms. The most careful dissection of the seed tells us little about the intricate splendour of the tree which actually confronts us, with its witness to the mysterious reality of life.

(2) This means that the material of the inquiry is not speculative and notional, but actual; 'is-ness,

not ought-ness '. No arid cleverness, no brainy theories, will ever show man the Reality of God or even the reality of his own soul. The only valid witness of the finite to the Infinite is the witness of real existents; and is experienced in 'that tough, bewildering yet immensely inspiring and truthfully testing thing, life as it is and as it surrounds us from the first '. To realize this fact of the mysterious ' richness of life ' around and within us was, he ever felt, the first step on the road to Reality.

(3) And, controlling our use of this living and present material, there is the never-to-be-forgotten fact of its closely knit organic character ; forbidding us to attach any ultimate reality to our neat divisions, abstract notions, diagrams and schemes, our arbitrary separation of ' sense ' from ' spirit ', ' thought ' from ' thing '. A profound consciousness of ' the strange but very certain and in the long run delightful interaction of any one thing with any thing else ' was fundamental to von Hügel's realistic outlook upon life. It gave a particular quality to his view of man's social, historical, and religious situation ; compelling breadth, suppleness and generosity, forbidding water-tight compartments, the deadly ' Either-Or ' of the exclusive mind, and all attempts to set up an opposition between visible and invisible religion, the logic of heart and of head. ' The penetration of spirit into sense, of the spaceless into space, of the Eternal into time, of God into man '—this he held to be the essential truth which Christianity revealed ; and it was a truth which he found fully operative on every level of existence.

I cannot but think that this intense consciousness

of the close-knit texture of our experience—the interpenetration of the realities within which we live and move—will come to be recognized as von Hügel's ruling intuition, and one of the chief contributions made by him to religious thought. Its influence is apparent in all his work, practical and philosophic. He was instinctively repelled by the closed system, the pietistic outlook, the ring-fenced soul: his world, whether seen in natural, social or spiritual regard, was full, rich, various, many-graded, living and organic through and through. All demand for clear definition, exclusive characters, hard edges—for 'pure' spirit, 'pure' experience, 'pure' thought and the rest—he regarded as the manifestation of a babyish arrogance; a shallow refusal to accept the reality of our human situation. That situation, as he saw it in its religious aspect, was summed up by him in a celebrated passage:

> Spirit and spirit, God and the creature, are not two material bodies, of which one can only be where the other is not; but, on the contrary, as regards our own spirit, God's Spirit ever works in closest penetration and stimulation of our own; just as, in return, we cannot find God's Spirit simply separate from our own spirit within ourselves. Our spirit clothes and expresses His; His Spirit first creates and then sustains and stimulates our own.

Entirely faithful to institutional Christianity in its most uncompromising form, it was largely on this doctrine of the interpenetration of realities that von Hügel's apologetic was built. For here he found a formula by which it was possible to justify the manifest dependence of man on the sensible and contingent, as the vehicle of the spiritual and abiding ; and explain the ruin which so commonly overtakes those who repudiate visible embodiments in favour of an entirely invisible religion. Sacraments, symbols, history and liturgy, ceremonial acts; all these, he felt, can and do convey in various degrees and ways the Reality of God to sense-conditioned creatures, and are discarded at our peril. We cannot safely comb out our complex being into separate strands, and set aside some as specially susceptible of the divine. Because 'Nature and Grace are closely inter-related parts of one great whole', the Supernatural, everywhere present, can and does reach us along sensible paths and awaken us by natural means. This, which represents one of von Hügel's deepest convictions, is of course the essence of the Catholic claim ; and it was put by him with unparalleled force.

> I kiss my child not only because I love it ; I kiss it also in order to love it. A religious picture not only expresses my awakened faith ; it is a help to my faith's awakening. . . . It is not magic, but a sheer fact traceable throughout our many-sided life, that we often grow, mentally and spiritually, almost solely by the stimulation of our senses or almost solely by the activity of other minds.

Nor is the power of conveying the Supernatural necessarily dependent on the precise quality and credentials of the conveying medium : which may and often does become penetrated by a significance undreamed by those who first devised it. The validity of the Christian sacraments is not threatened by even the most startling discoveries of comparative religion. Devotions which have no primitive sanction can yet convey the Supernatural, and so 'form saints and great saints'. The easy contempt of the educated mind for 'superstitions' is more often an evidence of shallowness than of depth. The spiritual treasure found in the Scriptures by 'humble tunnelling' is undamaged by the explorations of the Higher Criticism. It matters little that those Psalms which best evoke our sense of God were composed to meet special historic or liturgic requirements: since it is none the less true that 'precisely through these particular occasions of time and space, they succeeded in uttering the deepest and most universal aspirations of the heart towards God'. In Dante's picture of the ship of souls singing *In exitu Israel* as they sail towards the Mount of Purification, we have a perfect image of this fusion within man's spiritual life of historic, liturgic, and supersensual realities. Moreover this argument is not to be regarded as a mere piece of pragmatism; nor need we confine it to Christian practice alone. It has a universal validity within the lives of all God-seeking men, and helps us to understand the saints of other creeds. In all such cases, says von Hügel, 'what happens as a rule is simply this—the soul seeking God feeds upon such elements as it can assimilate in the tradition surrounding it; and divine grace under cover of these elements feeds and saves this soul'. They are in fact special instances of the interpenetration within our experience of natural and supernatural realities: the yeast of the Spirit ever at work in the dough of the common life, the simultaneous ever present in the successive.

The same principle governed the Baron's view of the

Church. He saw it not only as a mighty concrete institution within history; though this aspect, too, had for him great importance. It was to him, above all, 'a great hierarchy and *interconnection* of souls'; souls at every stage of growth and enlightenment, each with its own unexchangeable office, its own vocation and *attrait*, helping and completing one another. Each, so far as it was truly living, was growing up towards 'love, full being, and creative spiritual personality'; that type and degree of holiness wherein it could best contribute to the purposes of the whole.

> We all need one another . . . souls, all souls, are deeply interconnected. The Church at its best and deepest is just that—that interdependence of all the broken and meek, all the self oblivion, all the reaching out to God and souls . . . nothing is more real than this interconnection. We can suffer for one another . . . no soul is saved alone and by its own efforts.

Yet this interaction of souls, this mysterious but most actual Communion of Saints, depends for its life and reality on that deeper Life and Reality which penetrates and binds it in one—'The Sustainer and Filler of all that splendour . . . God, the great prevenient Spirit who works within and through this His kingdom of spirits'. And with these words, so characteristic in their fusion of the Personal and the Spaceless, we reach the fourth and all-embracing character of von Hügel's religious realism. The objective reality of finites, the genuine importance for us of the Here and Now, the Concrete, the Organic, rests on, is wholly immersed in, the Reality of all Realities; the personal and objective Being of God. No study of his mind and soul can be complete which does not lead up to this, his over-ruling intuition : the profound, adoring certitude of the Perfect, the Abiding, the Divine, as the Root of all Being, and the Fount of all joy.

What a happiness, what a joy it is to be *quite* sure that there is a God, not anything built up by mere human reasoning, no clever or subtle hypothesis, nothing particularly French or German or English, but something as infinitely more real than the air around us, and the pollen of the flowers, and the flight of the birds, and the trials and troubles and the needs of our little lives, stimulated and enriched by the lives of creatures so different from ourselves, touching us continually all round ; and the fundamental assurance is not simply one of variety or even of richness, it is an assurance accompanying and crowning all such sense of variety, of a reality, of the Reality, one and harmonious, strong and self-sufficing, of God.

This peculiar awareness of the Eternal seems to have been present in Friedrich von Hügel from childhood : and among the most illuminating passages in *The Reality of God* are those which reveal to us the close connexion between his final philosophic standpoint—apparently so closely reasoned, so well founded on history and psychology—and these innate dispositions. His immense influence as a religious thinker, which can be detected behind all the great movements of the religious soul in post-war Europe, is not in the last resort the influence of a great intellect. It derives from the rich and balanced vision, the experimental love, of a disciplined spiritual genius : characters which he has himself summed up as those of ' the moderate Theistic Christian mystic '.

At five and six years of age, I possessed a sense, not only of God in the external, especially the organic world, but of a mysterious divine Presence in the churches of Florence. Thus historical religion was with me, together with metaphysical (and natural) religion, from the first. . . . I remember very vividly how my delight was precisely in the fact that, beautiful as the external nature was, God did not consist even in its full totality, but was a Life, an Intelligence, a Love distinct from it all, in spite of His close penetration of it all. Thus Otherness was as [much] part of the outlook as was Reality.

In this vivid, first-hand sense of God's distinctness, which the Baron humbly believed that he 'shared with many another child', we can surely find the living germ from which his whole philosophy of religion arose. Developed and explicated under the two-fold influence of intellectual labour and spiritual experience, the immense attraction and authority of his teaching comes, more than all else, from the unmistakable note of awe-struck certitude which is heard whenever he turns from analysis to statement, from the doings of man to the Being of God. Other elements, ethical and historical, were added to the child's intuition. It was tested by much suffering and by the inevitable tension between the critical mind and the adoring soul. But it remained central; and is always present in those superb outbursts, full of tenderness and passion, which witness to the primacy of the Supernatural—or, as he loved to say, the 'Over-againstness of God'. These, revealing to us the heart of his faith and love, are the most truly significant utterances of the scholar-saint. Of his own soul at least, his contention was true, that religion is at bottom a 'metaphysical thirst'.

Those who are familiar with the religious currents in contemporary European life, tell us that the outstanding character of the most living Christianity is its revolt from subjectivity, its vigorous insistence on the objective and independent Reality of God, the Wholly Other. In their varying ways Otto, Barth, and Brunner, have developed and stressed this note with an exclusive intensity; placing the awe and abasement of the creature over against the unsearchable Divine Majesty—*Mysterium Tremendum et Fascinans*—in the forefront of their religious demand. 'Pure and exalted stands the power of God', says Barth, 'not beside, and not over, but on the other side of all conditioned-conditioning powers . . . the First and the Last, and as such the Unknown, but nowhere and never a Magnitude amongst others in the medium known to us.' No one can deny the value of this prophetic message, well named by its chief proclaimer a 'theology of correction'. It has restored to the Christian world that awe-struck upward glance, that sense of the Holy and the Transcendent, which is the salt of religion, and had nearly vanished beneath the floods of humanitarian piety.

Yet its almost inhuman other-worldliness, its contempt for 'religious experience', forms, ceremonies, and sacraments, have produced an inevitable reaction. The 'world-embracing temper' of Christian incarnational philosophy has reasserted itself. The delighted realization of God's self-revelation in Nature, and with this a fresh sense of the sacred character of physical and temporal life as the scene of the Christian triumph, are returning to their rightful place in the theological complex. To some extent the incarnational teaching of Father Lionel Thornton, and more fully that of the

Swedish theologians Nygren and Aulèn, with its emphasis on the Divine *Agape*, are here representative; but the spiritual life of young Germany, in so far as it is Christian, is strongly coloured by this circle of ideas. Last, in revolt from the arid intellectualism and the merely individualist outlook of the past generation, a deeper need for the organic, the institutional and the sacramental elements of religion has made itself felt. This is perhaps chiefly seen in the Catholic liturgic revival; but its influence is also recognizable in the Anglican Communion, and the chief reformed Churches of the Continent.

These three trends towards the transcendental, the incarnational, and the institutional, have appeared in distinct and even competitive forms. As a result, each has tended to a certain excess and want of balance; to the great detriment of religion as a whole. For all three are profoundly necessary to the rich totality of man's spiritual life; and should form a trinity in unity within which the soul matures. The awe-struck sense of the Eternal Perfect, the deep and tender love of natural life, the grateful use of Tradition and its embodiment in the Church, temper and reinforce each other. They form the triangular outline of the worshipping life. Yet it is strange that those who each pursue and proclaim one element, and forget, refuse, or minimize the rest, should ignore their synthesis in the work of the one great modern teacher of religion who has held in equal balance and humble reverence the reality of finites, and the Reality of God.

ADDITIONAL NOTE

BARON VON HÜGEL AS A SPIRITUAL TEACHER

IN one of his published writings, Baron von Hügel spoke of the many souls of every type with whom he had been brought into contact during his life ; and since those words were printed it is certain that their number must greatly have increased. Perhaps only those whose privilege it has been to be among them are in a position to suspect the amount of personal and devoted work, and that often of the most exacting kind, which lies behind this apparently simple phrase. 'One likes to help people ', was usually the only answer vouchsafed to the inarticulate but unmeasured gratitude of those whom he rescued from outer darkness, delivered by his own unique method from intellectual entanglements, and set firmly on their feet : thenceforward to prosecute a life which he never represented as anything less than 'costing '—one of his favourite words.

The great French religious renaissance of the seventeenth century—an epoch with which, as it seems to me, the Baron had certain temperamental links—was marked by the appearance of massive religious thinkers who were, at the same time, skilled directors of souls. This combination can also be detected in the Abbé Huvelin ; that 'manifestation of the spirit of sheer holiness ', whom Baron von Hügel regarded as his own supreme spiritual guide. It most certainly existed in the Baron himself ; and it is this power of holding, and practising together (in all their fullness and variety), the pastoral and the philosophic sides of the spiritual life, which made him, I believe without exception, the most influential religious personality of our time.

As with all the full-grown Christian mystics, that profound awareness of 'the august Object of religion', of which he has written so impressively, issued in his own case in a spiritual creativeness; a capacity for reaching, penetrating, vivifying souls, which did not stop short with those who knew him in the flesh. 'He was like a rock to me', wrote one who had never known him personally, on receiving the news of his death. 'He said the things I had listened for so long. With him, one was safe and certain.' The full number of his spiritual children will never be known; nor the extent to which his generously given advice, teaching and support are ultimately destined to fertilize the most distant corners of the Christian field. His great sanctity—for no one could ever have heard him speak of God without being profoundly changed by that experience—his fearless intellectual outlook, the ease and suppleness with which he ranged from the loftiest peaks to the homeliest duties of religion, and a power of 'discerning spirits' which was often extremely disconcerting to its victims, produced in him just that 'spiritual persuasiveness' which he recognized and so deeply admired in St. Catherine of Genoa. Such persuasiveness—such a power of convincing other souls of the reality and loveliness of God—requires, he thought

> A life sufficiently large and alive to take up and retain, within its own experimental range, at least some of the poignant question and conflict, as well as of the peace-bringing solution and calm; hence a life dramatic with a humble and homely heroism which in rightful contact with, and in rightful renunciation of, the Particular and Fleeting, ever seeks and

finds the Omnipresent and Eternal; and which again deepens and incarnates (for its own experience and apprehension, and for the stimulation of other souls) this Transcendence in its own thus gradually purified Particular: only such a life can be largely persuasive, at least for us Westerns and in our times.

And here the many who owe to him their peace of mind and such usefulness as they possess, may feel that he has drawn his own portrait.

In his practical dealings with souls, the Baron was accustomed to apply under modern conditions many of the salient ideas of the great French directors; especially Fénelon, whom he greatly admired. Their robust outlook, their hatred of self-occupation and scrupulosity, their insistence on moderation and balance, were all echoed by him. 'Solid, simple, sober souls' were the type he most approved, and sought to form. The 'mystical element' of religion was never allowed to dominate the field, or become the one basis of faith. Our poor little human experience of Reality, he taught, must always fluctuate; and have its uncertainties even at the best. But 'God and Christ and the need of our constant death to self, remain *simply certain*'. Hence self-abandonment was the crowning virtue; and 'humbling and bracing' were the twin qualities he looked for in spiritual reading and prayer. Any display of vehemence or feverish intensity was likely to be met by a humiliating request to 'try a little gardening', or, in female patients, 'some quiet needlework'; for secular interests and employments took a prominent place in his conception of the ordered spiritual life, as we may see in the passage devoted to this matter in the great final chapter of *The Mystical Element*. Moreover, such an ordered life invariably included some care for, and, if possible, direct intercourse with, the poor; since the Baron strongly believed—in a way not well understood by the modern social worker—in their humbling and spiritualizing influence. 'God, Christ and the Poor' is a trilogy that occurs frequently in his private correspondence: as does the steady insistence on every form and degree of homely love:

> I deeply love my little dog; and Abbé Huvelin was devoted to his cat. We can and will become all the dearer to God for this our love of our little relations, the smaller children of God.

'How *great* if you could end by a certain real interest in those "nothings", an interest springing from the purest love of those souls!' he once wrote to one who had betrayed exasperation with the petty details of life: and this chance phrase seems to me to throw a flood of light on his conception of the line along which that 'purification and expansion of the soul' which he desired, could best be achieved, and man draw nearer to likeness with God.

The same breadth, charity, and common sense, the same dislike of strain and excess, entered into his treatment of the doctrinal problems which play so large a part in modern religious unrest. 'Let it alone—feed your soul on the great positive truths you *do* see.' As for the apparently indigestible morsels, the incipient controversialist was warned against all hurried denunciation, since 'They may be food for other souls, and perhaps even for *yours*, in a later stage of its growth!'—a prophecy which was often enough fulfilled. Many have been saved from theological suicide by these wise counsels: the more impressive because coming from a great scholar, who had himself faced every scientific and critical difficulty, yet remained a devoted son of the Roman Catholic Church.

In the advice and training which he gave so generously to many outside his own communion, he showed the fullest willingness to use, discriminate, and take seriously the institutional practices of all branches of the Church. Anything and everything offering deliverance from that pantheistic and unitarian trend which he specially abhorred in modern religious thought, anything which would convert 'abstractions floating in the air' into the constituents of 'a Reality felt and loved', was seriously considered by him. Though there were extreme developments of Anglo-Catholic practice which he certainly regarded with mingled amusement and regret, he viewed with thankfulness 'the most true and precious beliefs' involved in the Anglican trend towards increased sacramentalism, advised and upheld frequent and regular communion, and also approved the custom of prayer before the Reserved Sacrament: since this devotion, though not primitive, 'had formed saints, and great saints'. Here shows that strongly practical bent which entered in a marked degree into the Baron's view of institutional practices: and which appears in a classic form in the systems of the great spiritual directors, such as S. François de Sales. This is merely to say in other words that his supreme interest here lay in souls and their growth—in arousing the deepest reality of man to the overwhelming Reality, the richness and attraction of God—and that he recognized, and valued, many diverse means as serving this great end. It was because of his own deep, awed consciousness of that unchangeable End, 'present, yet absent—near, yet far', that he was able to persuade others to seek it: even along paths which the modern spirit is apt to despise. God—adoration—self-oblivion—surrender: these keywords of religion, and beyond these, even such purely technical terms as ontology or transcendence, became, when he uttered them, incandescent with a supernatural fire. A letter written by him in the last All Saints' tide of his life, ended upon the words —'Full of the breadth, the depth, and the tenderness of the Saints.' Those who owe him most, will see in this phrase his fitting epitaph.

Ingram Content Group UK Ltd.
Milton Keynes UK
UKHW021831030423
419563UK00011B/1649